Bologna Reflections

By the Same Author

Travelers Tales San Francisco: *Dreaming of Muir Woods*

30 Days in Italy: *The Gift*

A Woman's World Again: *Leila's Gesture*

Bologna Reflections

An Uncommon Guide

Mary Tolaro Noyes

Jump The Fence Press

Contributors

All drawings and watercolors – Philip W. Noyes
Photographs, including cover design – Mary Tolaro Noyes
Graphic Assistance – Sean Roherty, Philip W. Noyes
Layout, Design, Maps – Thomas J. Noyes
Cover Photograph – Canale Navile – Mary Tolaro Noyes
Back Photograph – detail from *Madonna del Terremoto* – Mary Tolaro Noyes
Italian Translations – Mary Tolaro Noyes
Proofreaders – Pamela Lawrence, Diletta Torlasco

ISBN 978-0-578-01683-2

Jump The Fence Press
www.jumpthefencepress.com

For Tom

Acknowledgements

Special thanks to my husband Tom Noyes. Without his unfailing assistance, BOLOGNA REFLECTIONS would not exist. I cannot imagine this book without the drawings and paintings of our son Philip. From the beginning his collaboration has been crucial. To my parents Philip and Rita Tolaro and to Jim, Angie, Karen, and Melissa I offer thanks for their help and encouragement.

I dedicate BOLOGNA REFLECTIONS to Luisa Castelli's memory (1904–2006). She shared both her love and her Bolognese family with me. In particular, I offer sincere gratitude to Emanuela Casanova, Emanuele and Paola Casanova, Ettore and Paola Casanova, Clara Castelli and Renato Zagatti, and Cesare and Bruna Trancolin.

Thank you to my friends, both Bolognese and American, who kept me focused on the project. Mille grazie to Paolo and Bruna Fornasiero, Anna Maria Grandi and family, Mimma Marchetti, and Laura Pergola, whose friendship and knowledge have nurtured me in my search for Bologna's soul. Thanks also to the International Women's Forum of Bologna, to Massimo Maracci and the Cultura Italiana Language School, and to all the wonderful Bolognese people who shared their lives. Special thanks to Sarah and Jack Blanshei, scholars and friends who have been so generous, and to Sally Hudson, Peggy Kidney, Nan McElroy, Erin Hogan, and Elizabeth Robinson for their enthusiasm and willingness to help.

Contents

Images

Preface

My discovery of Bologna began in 1994. I had previously sat in a train compartment at Bologna Centrale, like many other visitors to Italy, waiting for passengers to disembark and embark, anxious to hurry on to Roma, Firenze, or Venezia. From the train window Bologna never inspired a visit. Boxy buildings covered with wide-angled, gaudy graffiti lined the rails that ease into the station, while train tracks crisscrossed to the right and left, wires stretched out overhead, and typical concrete platforms edged each side of the tracks. People milled about waiting for a train, for someone. Even the landscape outside the train window on the outskirts of the city remained largely uninspiring.

When I decided to improve my Italian to facilitate communicating with the newly discovered family in Sicily, I asked the counsel of an Italian professor. He suggested seeking a school in Bologna, a place not overrun by tourists, whose people would be welcoming. I followed his advice and, besides learning the language, I discovered the treasures of a remarkable city.

Now when arriving by train, I look eagerly for clues that Bologna is close at hand. The city's colors, shades of golden ocher and rust, tint the rectangular country houses and palazzi in the peripheral towns just as they color the city itself.

I cannot imagine why the regular rows of trellised grapevines that fill the fields on either side of the train did not evoke anticipation before. One time I remember leaving Bologna in late December on a nearly empty train, a mixture of cold rain and snow falling on black vines and the black earth outside, as we sped toward Milano in late afternoon. The surreal world outside the window matched my sad mood as I left behind my Italian life.

In springtime though, soft pink wildflowers poke up between the rows of freshly tilled earth. Young shoots of green new growth on the grapevines twine arduously around the trellis wires stretched between them. The leafy vines turn the world green in summer and gold and russet as the season bends toward autumn and the harvest.

And how could I have ignored the green, sweetly undulating hills to the south, with their promise of the Apennines rising toward Tuscany? Or the graceful cupola of the Santuario di San Luca as I sat on the train approaching from Milano? The snaking portico allows the pilgrim to climb up the Colle della Guardia, from the Meloncello to the sanctuary outside the city limits, protected from the elements.

When I refer to discovering Bologna, I admit to an ongoing seduction by her unique past and modern charm, not the least of which are the Bolognesi themselves. Emanuela will be there, Paolo and Bruna, Clara and Renato, Anna Maria, Mimma, Cesare and Bruna, the couple at the market, as well as all the other nameless merchants who always remember me on my return. Now each trip to Italy includes a stop in the Città Rossa, but not merely in a train compartment at a *binario* at Bologna Centrale, on the way to somewhere else.

This book is the record of my discoveries, often the result of sharing life with generous and friendly people. The modern charm of the city complements well the magic of her past, and perhaps you will also be seduced.

Read BOLOGNA REFLECTIONS before you go to whet the appetite for the feast when you arrive. Use BOLOGNA REFLECTIONS as a loose guide while you are there, to discover the city's hidden treasures—both mine and yours. Read BOLOGNA REFLECTIONS after your sojourn has ended, to experience the city again, her medieval magic and modern charm, and then perhaps begin planning your next visit.

~

About the Author   Mary Tolaro Noyes was raised in Bellows Falls, Vermont, where her Sicilian grandparents settled in the early twentieth century. She and her husband Tom live in San Francisco, California. After years dedicated to raising two sons and to teaching, Mary has finally come to the writing she always meant to do. Inspired by rediscovering her grandparents' families in Sicily in 1989, she first visited Bologna in 1994 as a student of Italian. After frequent extended stays, Mary has come to regard the Città Rossa as her second home and is still taken by the city's medieval magic and modern charm.

~

About the Artist   Philip Noyes teaches Art at Burlingame High School, near San Francisco, California. He lived and studied in Italy for six months and did many of the drawings and watercolors while in Bologna. Philip now specializes in ceramics and has developed a Computer Art course for high school students.

iv

A Walking Guide

for Bologna Reflections

Maps

Legend

Start: ★

Stop: ●

Wander: ● . . . ●

Turn: ↺↻

Follow: ➡

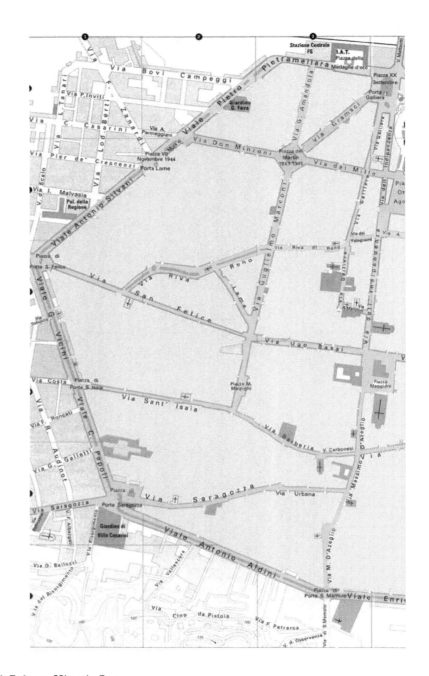

Figure 1. Bologna Historic Center

vi

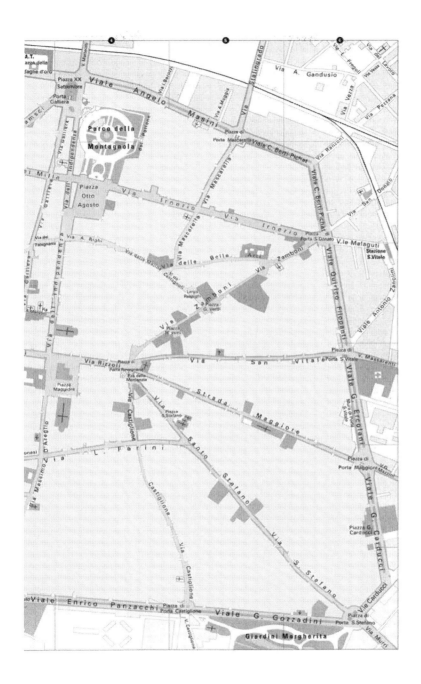

Discovering

Figure 2. Piazza di Porta Ravegnana, Drawing after Theopile Gautier

Bologna Is . . .

Bologna is light slashed

By twelfth century towers,

Casting shadows on life's surface,

Shadows whose shapes

Can hide the hidden treasures of the past,

The promise of today.

Bologna is colors

Seeping into the consciousness,

Until the world is shades of ocher and gold,

Violet, rose and gray,

Russet and the red of

Tiled roofs and clay bricks.

Bologna is porticoed, serpentine forms

And jagged fragments,

Layers and veils.

Bologna is seductive, gentle.

Bologna is . . .

Figure 3. Representation of Bologna in Piazza Galileo

So That's Where I Was

We leaned our bikes up against the concrete fence running along the edge of the canal and crossed over a rickety metal-plate bridge to a cement island in the middle of the waterway. Electric wires crisscrossed above us. The towers connecting them straddled overgrown shrubs and weeds. A group of five Sunday afternoon cyclists, we were searching for the hidden canals of Bologna's past.

The funny thing was that the colors, sounds, and smells were unexpectedly familiar. My companions were busy discussing the Canale Navile's northern escape from the perimeter of the old city, but the musty smell of the brackish water and its slow trickle and splash reminded me of my first day in Bologna a year and a half earlier. "So that's where I was."

~

March 19, 1994

I arrived on a train from Milano just before eleven a.m. on a Saturday, with too many bags and instructions to look for a short, dark-haired woman dressed in red, the landlady of the apartment I would rent in Bologna for two

5

months while studying Italian. She would give me the keys and the address, and I could begin my adventure. Honestly, I hoped that was the plan. Our phone conversation the night before had left me confused. Blaring traffic outside the phone booth in Milano and her answering machine's scratchy message playing its muddled refrain underneath our conversation had interfered as she warned me of the problems concerning my arrival. The details remained hazy. After all I was there to learn Italian, and evidently she did not understand English.

She had said that we should meet, not at the main exit of Bologna Centrale but at the exit near the telephones. However, when I arrived at the station, I found signs for three exits. Flights of stairs threatened from each direction but neither elevator nor banks of carts proffered help. Choosing a direction with no visible steps, I struggled along the corridor, following the crowd and the signs for *Uscita Ovest* (west exit). A flight of roughly fifteen steps suddenly confronted me at the end of the hallway. "Whew, am I really going to need all these books to get through the Italian classes?" I thought.

With my computer bag crisscrossed over my chest and a carry-on slung over my left shoulder, I hauled the overstuffed black duffle up the stairs, along with my backpack, and then hustled back down to the bottom, took a deep breath, and dragged the biggest suitcase up one step at a time.

Looking exactly like the classic inexperienced traveler, I pushed the book-heavy duffle along the shiny marble floor toward the exit. When I discovered a whole room of public telephones near the door, relief replaced apprehension. Perhaps I had found the appointed meeting place by chance. It felt great to be confident about something.

At the curb outside I organized the bags and suitcases into a neat pile and collapsed. It was 11:10. Then I waited—and waited—and waited and—worried, because I knew from our conversation that the Signora had an appointment at half past eleven. "Where is she?" I thought, "and what will I do if she doesn't show up?"

The frenetic coming and going of Saturday travelers at Bologna Centrale kept me busy examining signoras of the appropriate age. Most did not match the voice I had heard over the phone: feisty and solicitous, yes—forget matronly and demure! So I waited and watched, afraid to move, afraid to miss her looking for me. At one point I stood up and walked around, agitated and tired. Back and forth, back and forth.

"I need a plan," I decided. "I'll wait here until noon. If she doesn't show up, I'll store my suitcases at the baggage depository and try to find a hotel." I only wanted to get somewhere to sleep and gather my scattered self. "I'm not in the mood for misadventures," I lamented. The school, which had arranged for the lodging, had not given me an emergency contact number or offered a contingency plan. I knew they were closed on Saturday, so I was on my own.

Well on the way toward frenzy, I finally saw her. Absolutely no doubt about it. Smart looking, short, slender, with shoulder-length hair styled in a neat pageboy. She wore a very proper gold and red plaid blazer with an apple-red dress and black pumps. The red beret was angled nattily on her gyrating head, while her black eyes darted from person to person. When our eyes connected, we knew.

Deep creases ringed her large, dark eyes and already-wagging mouth. We greeted each other formally in Italian. Then she continued the conversation at me. I understood maybe half of what she was saying. Key words stood out: The *appartamento* is not available. You're at the wrong *uscita*. I cannot carry the *valige*. It was just noon.

Bologna Reflections

I asked her for the keys and address. She responded that the apartment was not available, believing that talking louder and faster would help me better understand the circumstances. Suddenly she zipped off toward the crowd of mopeds, cars, buses, and scurrying people, her response tossed back over her left shoulder. I decided to stay put. She had lost herself so quickly in the confusion that following her was not really an option. I hoped she was going to get the luggage cart I had not been able to find. She had said something about a motorino. "Maybe that's the word for luggage cart," I thought.

Perhaps ten minutes later, she approached slowly, beret now askew, dragging her motorino, which didn't want to start. "No luggage cart," I deduced. The black, beat-up moped had an oversized plastic windshield that threatened to blow away like a sail. She staggered up beside me, still explaining that she could not carry my suitcases, as if she'd been talking to me the whole time. I kept asking, "But Signora, is there a place for me to sleep tonight?" Obviously, neither of us was listening.

Finally I said, "Signora, I will take a taxi. You don't have to carry my bags. Just tell me the address and give me the keys, and I'll go wherever." (Perhaps I was not quite so direct with my spotty Italian.) In the meantime, I began to carry the suitcases toward the taxi line ten feet away and a driver came forward to help. She scooted in behind us, explaining that she didn't know the address of the apartment and couldn't give me the keys because.... She would lead on motorino and the taxi driver would follow. He seemed neither surprised nor perturbed by the request. His agreeability rubbed off on me, so I climbed into the back seat, relaxed ever so slightly, and waited for them to finish.

When he hopped in the driver's seat, he looked back at me, shook his head, mumbling something under his breath. Then he waited for the Signora to retrieve her motorino and take off. She did, with a wave of her arm. We followed her into the whizzing traffic on Viale Pietro Pietramellara, but she

8

nudged along slowly, too slowly, on one of the busiest streets in Bologna. Her motorino was not the kind that zooms, buzzing loudly as it explodes down the street. She putted, and we putted too. The driver muttered, and so it went. She sat erect on the seat of her battered vehicle, her perfect, pert, pageboy coif immobile, the straight red dress hiked high up on her thighs, the proper black pumps hooked over the vibrating peddles, the flimsy windshield flapping happily in the cool March breeze.

I could tell we were not going toward the historic center. We passed the railroad yard with its high fences, stationary railroad cars, warehouses, and piles of tracks. Then we entered an industrial neighborhood with boxy, modern apartment buildings interspersed among warehouses. "This is charming, medieval Bologna?" I thought. My heart sank and the tired stupor vanished. "Where is she putting me?" I pleaded, to no one in particular. "Where are the towers and the porticoes, Piazza Maggiore?" My first night in Bologna was not going to be what I had expected.

~

She was in a hurry, having already missed her appointment: a friend's wedding. She led me up the steps of a tired old mustard-gold palazzo. In the complex of dreary, drab warehouses, it was the only habitable building. Concrete and cinderblock surrounded it and tall, straggly weeds poked up here and there between cracks in the pavement. I waited while she jiggled the key in the lock of the well-worn, heavy wooden door, which finally creaked open. I pushed my bags along the marble floor of the dark corridor and up to the first door on the left, as she tried key after key, all the while mumbling. When she finally found the key, she practically pushed me inside the door, as it scraped open unwillingly. Her eyes were darting around the whole time, as if she expected someone to jump out of the cupboards and find us out.

"Signora," she said, agitated but trying to act calm, her voice even and unhurried as her body itched to get away. "I am late for my appointment and will have to leave you here and return later to explain everything. Please, you shouldn't disrupt anything?" she questioned, more than admonished.

"Can I at least make the bed and take a nap?" I ventured bravely. "I am very tired from the long trip."

"Well," she said, "yes, I guess so. You can take a nap, but only on the sofa here. Don't use the sheets. No. No, don't make up the bed. I'll bring you sheets when I come back in a few hours."

She handed me the keys and flew out the door, adding as an afterthought, "If you want to eat you should go to the market on Via Ugo Bassi to buy some food. Remember, the stores will close at one p.m."

I stood there in the dark apartment, all the shutters closed tightly against would-be intruders, and wondered where I was. Resigned and confused, I closed the door and opened the squeaky windows with their peeling green shutters that faced the driveway. Sunlight streamed in and transformed the space into a cozy nest. It clearly belonged to an artist, given the posters and artwork decorating the walls and the easel in the loft. I went to the kitchen window that faced out back and opened it and its shutters as well.

A smallish river meandered slowly under an arched stone overpass some distance to the left. I wondered again where I was, where the twelfth-century towers were, and what I was doing surrounded by industrial warehouses next to a murky waterway.

I went into the tiny living room and flopped onto the flowery red couch, the gentle sounds of the water soothing me. When I looked at my watch

I realized that in less than an hour it would be too late to get food. However, I first needed to figure out where I was.

I grabbed my purple backpack, the Italy guidebook with the unspecific Bologna map, the keys, and left. Once outside, I crossed the deserted parking lot and walked toward Via Bovi Campeggi. I got lost on the way to Via dell'Indipendenza but then flew under its broad porticoes toward what I hoped would be Via Ugo Bassi and the market. I arrived at the foot of the wide street out of breath and relieved by my first success: I had found Via Ugo Bassi. A line snaked around the corner where a McDonald's served up its fare and I thought, "Oh no, I didn't come here for this! There goes my romantic image of Bologna." I didn't even notice the Asinelli and Garisenda towers to the left or Neptune's fountain across the street, directly in front of me.

I turned right onto Via Ugo Bassi, past the McDonald's, and scurried along, looking for the market. I only found clothing stores, a pharmacy, and bars. I worried, "What will I do if I can't find any food to buy? Will I be relegated to McDonald's?"

Finally, after five minutes that seemed like fifteen, I saw the half-hidden entrance into the Mercato delle Erbe. It was not a supermarket, as I had expected, but a gigantic gallery of small farmers' stalls with fruit, vegetables and other food items—along with a cacophony of talking and dealing shoppers.

"O Lord," I thought, "I have only fifteen minutes, where do I begin?" I wasn't in the mood for exploring, but I told myself to either get moving or go hungry. The next day would be Sunday with few options for purchasing food. I threw myself into shopping with only a few minutes to spare, not believing the huge space had completely emptied in fifteen minutes. I felt successful, and ready to get back to the apartment to make lunch.

Bologna Reflections

And what a great tuna and chopped fennel sandwich I made, with a thick slice of tomato. While I sat there in someone's kitchen eating, I resolved to enjoy the adventure that the next two months in Bologna would bring. Euphoria set it and I saw myself a protagonist in an Italian film. The apartment felt like home already. Books everywhere. Black and white Pier Paolo Pasolini posters. The gaunt, sad face of the poet-film director looked out at me, while I looked deeper into the life of my unknown host. More books. No television. High, very high ceilings. White wallpaper with light blue dots the size of quarters, dimes, and peas all trimmed in violet. More posters. The bed, together with a dresser, filled the welcoming lofted space back behind the couch.

After eating I curled up like a dozing kitty on the couch and tried to read. However, my eyes kept closing, so I ignored the Signora's warning and found some sheets, made up the bed, and slept. The phone's insistent r-i-n-g, r-i-n-g woke me about half past three.

I stumbled to the phone, picked up the receiver tentatively, and said "pronto." I was hoping that it was the Signora and not some unknown person who would hurry into a long discourse in colloquial Italian. Relieved to recognize her voice, I explained that she didn't have to bring sheets and towels because I had found the sheets and I had my own towel. However, in about twenty minutes she arrived on her motorino.

We chatted, half in English, half in Italian. "Signora, Mary," she greeted me when I opened the door. "Come stai? Posso darti del tu?" she added quickly before I could even say that I was fine. She was evidently anxious to move from formal to informal conversation by asking my permission right away.

I responded "Sì, sì" and noticed that she had changed from her bright tailored jacket and dress to casual around-the-house brown slacks and a saggy beige sweater. The hat was gone, too, and an old brown jacket hung low on her shoulders. Upon entering, she gave the space a cursory once-over.

We removed the sheets from the bed and replaced them with hers. In English she said, as she smiled in a friendly manner, "May-ry, I am 'appy that you are 'ere, and American. I don't meet Americans." She had thought I was going to be German and seemed really pleased to have an American tenant, especially one from California. "I have been to California," she added. "I will tell you about it one day."

"I would like to hear the story soon," I answered, in English as well. "I will invite you to my 'ouse very soon," she countered, "maybe tomorrow, and we can visit." "Grazie Signora, mi piacerebbe molto, I would like that," I said.

Then she added, "I tink you will need a bicicletta to go to the school from the apartment—I will find one for you." "Thank you, that would be helpful," I responded, wondering how in the world I would manage in the city's roiling traffic.

When we finished making the bed she said, "Tomorrow afternoon about one p.m. I will come and get you and bring you to your apartment. Okay? Tutto okay?" And, without a second's hesitation, I declared, "Sì, sì, tutto okay." As I closed and locked the door behind her I realized, surprised, that I liked her.

I read and dozed for the next few hours, too tired to explore the city. I gazed out the kitchen window at the tranquil river. I listened to the water running by and wondered about it, where it was from, where it went. I didn't feel alone, even if I was, in that isolated, strange but charming place. "What will tomorrow bring?" I asked myself as I turned out the light and snuggled down into the covers. "I'm here until I hear from the Signora. I'm very happy," I admitted. The sound of running water outside the window kept me company as I drifted down into a deep and, surprisingly, restful sleep.

~

The next day she did come, but not until six p.m., when suddenly the doorbell rang and she was there with a friend and a car to take me to my official apartment. She hurried in, all the time mumbling to her friend. They whipped the sheets off the bed and folded them quickly. The Signora looked around sizing-up the condition of the place, the question "Does it look like someone has been here?" nagging at her conscience, I knew.

Later I understood my landlady's ways, the wheeling, dealing and machinations that turned simple situations into complicated and sometimes messy ones. She had made me wait for my already-reserved apartment because a woman had decided to leave on Sunday instead of the promised Saturday, allowing her to collect an extra day's rent payment. Our tenant-landlady relationship continued over the next two months, always full of surprises. I never did get to her house to eat, although I knew her intentions were good. Life just seemed to get in the way of tomorrow's plans. By the time I left she was in a leg cast because of an accident on her motorino.

~

October 8, 1995

"So this is where I was," I said to the group as we stood there trying to piece together the puzzle of Bologna's once watery history. We were standing at the Bova, the city's ancient port, where the waterways that meandered around inside Bologna since the Middle Ages joined together and exited away from the city toward the Po and Ferrara, Venezia, and the Adriatic. They laughed at the irony of my being familiar with a place none of them had ever known before. I marveled at that first welcome to Bologna by the Signora, whose friend never knew that a stranger had moved into her apartment for a day and a half.

When I returned to Bologna about a year later, I saw her zip by on a flashy new motorino, dressed in shiny black leather from head to toe: hat, body-hugging short jacket, tight pants, and tall, sleek boots. Our eyes connected for an instant, shocked at recognizing each other. I continued on my way as she zoomed off in the opposite direction, carried by the uncompromising flow of noontime traffic. Little did I know then, however, that the Signora and I were destined to intercept each other's lives again—but that is another story.

Figure 4. Canale Navile from Via Piella

The Story of Bologna's Waterways

Along the banks of canals that have traversed Bologna under the open sky for centuries, were the silk and flour mills and small factories that cured skins and tobacco, made paper, dyed cloth, and worked metal. They depended on the canals to produce the energy created by a water wheel to process their goods. That hidden city of underground canals and natural waterways is one voice of Bologna's past.

Evidence exists of Roman engineering designed to harness the power of the waterways near Bologna in the fifth century AD. The Reno, the river to west of the city, was diverted shortly after 1000 AD to form the Canale del Reno, which connected Corticella, just a few miles north, with Ferrara, near the Adriatic coast. The transport of goods was a major use of the canal.

Government documents show that during the following decades, great interest grew for a new system of locks for the Reno River at Casalecchio that would carry the water to Bologna, as it still does today. An exact history has not yet been documented, but it seems that in 1208 the Comune of Bologna constructed the new lock. After entering the city at the Grada, it joined the Cerchia del Mille near the Serraglio del Poggiale, once a *porta* (city gate) near the intersection of Via Riva di Reno and today's Via Marconi. Then it divided into two branches. One named Canale Cavaticcio went north to the ports of Maccagnano (1284), known today as the Bova, and Corticella. From the Bova to

Bologna Reflections

Corticella, the waterway became the Canale Navile. It is not clear if ships reached the city's wall or if they stopped outside at the two ports.

Meanwhile, the second branch of the Canale del Reno went for a distance along the city's moat, forming an added degree of defense and serving as a primitive sewer system. It continued on to Via Falegnami, crossed Via Piella and, at Via Oberdan, divided into two branches. One branch went directly north and was known as the Canale delle Moline because of the flour mills that it drove. It straddled Via Capo di Lucca and Via del Pallone, at the city wall, then joined the Torrente Aposa to go to the Bova where it flowed into the Canale Navile.

In 1221 the city constructed the Canale di Savena at the locks of San Ruffillo. It approached the city through the Giardini Margherita where it fed its little lake. The canal entered into Bologna from Porta Castiglione and headed north to the ancient *torresotto* (a city gate with passageway). It went under the Teatro Duse and then along the streets that were once the moat of the Cerchia del Mille: Rialto, Cartoleria, Guerazzi, Piazza Aldrovandi, Petroni, Castagnoli, and Moline, where it then flowed into the Torrente Aposa.

The Torrente Aposa, the only natural waterway that traversed Bologna, approached it from Via San Mamolo and entered at the ancient Serraglio dell'Aposa, passed behind the church of San Domenico, then flanked Via Castiglione, crossed Piazza Minghetti, Via Clavature, and Via Rizzoli. Next it bordered Via dell'Inferno and crossed Piazza San Martino. It then edged Via Capo di Lucca, where it mingled with the Canale delle Moline near the city wall and the Montagnola.

The names of some medieval streets hark back to the canals and their economic relevance in Bologna: Via Altaseta (silk), Via Arienti (silver), Via dell'Oro (gold), Via Cartoleria (paper), Via Coltelli (knives), Via Coltellini (little knives), Via delle Moline (flour mills); even Via Riva di Reno refers to the canal and its banks as it flowed through the city from the west and then curved north.

Bologna's system of waterways linked her to the Po River and the Adriatic Sea during the Middle Ages, which was the principal route for the importation of grain from Romagna. It also had important political ramifications for the city and its relationships with Ferrara and Venezia. We could have begun a sea voyage to the exotic Orient in Bologna, far away from the sea. Visits to the Chiusa at Casalecchio and the Museo del Patrimonio Industriale (Via della Beverara 123) provide visual images and explain the waterways and their use in the city over the centuries.

Figure 5. In the Shadows Under Bologna's Porticoes

Com'è Bella! Life Under Bologna's Porticoes

"**B**uona sera, signora!" he greeted me, his voice inflected up in pleasure, as he broke his long, fast stride unexpectedly. The gentleman from the small bank on Strada Maggiore, who always changed my dollars into *lire* and managed a friendly conversation, was hurrying home from work. His right hand reached out to meet mine in salutation under the broad portico between Santa Maria dei Servi and Palazzo Hercolani.

I had been doing my usual late afternoon shopping in Piazza Aldrovandi and carried bags filled with fresh vegetables and fruit, cheese, bread, and wine. "Buona sera," I replied, startled at being recognized by someone in the rushing crowd. We stood among groups of congregating students from the Department of Political Science, which occupies Palazzo Hercolani, and a bank of parked motorini. The traffic whizzed by, its racket echoing underneath the portico as we chatted.

"How's your book coming?" he questioned with a smile. I explained my research, which centered on the basilica of Santo Stefano. He smiled and shook his head, clearly pleased as I described my insights into a place that the Bolognesi hold sacred.

Then we laughingly segued into our other main topic of conversation. "How are your English lessons going?" I ventured.

Bologna Reflections

"Mary," he responded, because we had switched to our usual informal rapport, "I understand well enough when the teacher speaks, but I still can't force myself to say anything, in case I will make a mistake."

"Yes, I understand," I rejoined, "you don't mind deciphering my Italian, including *my* mistakes, but you have to be perfect before you'll converse in English!"

"You're right," he admitted, "but I'm working on it. I guess I'll need to put extra effort into the lessons in order to read your book. I have to see what an American writes about my city!" he added with a smile.

"Don't worry," I teased, as we waved good-bye to each other and went off in opposite directions.

~

A walk under Bologna's porticoes tends to be like that, even for a visitor like me. There is always a friendly glance, an animated greeting, a firm handshake. A merchant or clerk outside an oft-frequented shop or office recognizes me and a conversation ensues. The portico is an extension of the home, market, or office, full of bustling foot traffic at certain times of the day. Often no walls separate the life inside from that outside during the hectic morning rush, the late morning visit to the nearby bar, the early evening shopping and socializing, and the even later exit to a restaurant or concert. Porticoes connect every aspect of life to its next stop. Sometimes elegant, sometimes crowded, sometimes dark and narrow, and yes, sometimes dirty and noisy, they are as familiar and comfortable as home.

Nevertheless it's easy to take them for granted, to walk, eyes focused a step away instead of running along the ribbon of walkway that stretches out toward the distant swatch of brilliant sky. It's easy to take advantage of the comfort they provide and neither search for hidden treasures in the niches and angles nor gaze at the shadows casting shapes on the stone pavement while the sun fulfills its daily rounds. It's easy to say to oneself "Yes, aren't the porticoes interesting" and not search underneath the reality of their physical presence to understand the uniqueness and spirit of Bologna, a city of porticoes since the thirteenth century.

Porticoes did not originate in Bologna. The idea of outside protection from the elements was not a new one. The Roman maenianum, a wooden extension that overhung the street from the second floor of the insulae, their block-long apartment-like complexes, could be considered a precursor. Religious abbeys like Santo Stefano and San Procolo sprung up in and around medieval Bologna, as in other European cities, and local artisans built their cloisters, which were not only inspiring places to meditate but also practical against inclement weather.

Merchants in the twelfth century often attached tent-like awnings to their house or storefront, which extended out over the street and protected them from rain, snow, and hot sun while they worked. Because their stalls were up close to the edifice for stability, the covering became a natural way to protect them and their clients while they crafted and sold their wares. The portico seems a logical improvement over that practice.

In 1230, as the population of Bologna doubled, students continued to arrive from around the world to study at the already famous university. The medieval walled city was not able to accommodate the constant influx, and a law was promulgated that allowed a property owner who took in a student to extend the wall facing the street outward to increase the space in his home by almost four feet. Medieval passageways were narrow, with no room for expansion at the street level. Bologna's early landlords pushed the wall out one floor up, so that it hung out over the public lane. One thing led to another, of course. Eventually, what began as a little push outward became a bigger extension. Soon oak trunks on pedestals of gypsum were required to support the weight of the bulge. The "portico Bolognese" was born.

A group of houses on Via Clavature (16–18) illustrates the development of the portico from its ancestor, the bulge. Casa Isolani in Strada Maggiore (19), Casa Grassi in Via Marsala (12), and Casa Rampionesi-Reggiani in Via del Carro (4) are examples of the earliest porticoes with their tree-trunk supports. The Orphanage of San Leonardo (fourteenth century) at Via Begatto 17 is another ancient, porticoed house. Eventually wood was abandoned in favor of bricks and stone after terrible fires destroyed many edifices.

A number of thirteenth century statutes regulated the building and maintenance of porticoes. In 1249 it was decreed that the height from the ground had to be seven feet so that a man on horseback could pass comfortably underneath. In 1289 a law mandated that the proprietor of any house in Bologna without a portico had to construct one. It further declared that the maintenance of the private space fell to him, although he must allow public passage. Bologna's solutions for maintaining and regulating her characteristic porticoes still function in a similar manner today.

~

And I have a wealth of memories to share after walking under Bologna's nearly twenty-five miles of porticoes for many years.

The broad, elegant ones of Via dell'Indipendenza and the Portico del Pavaglione are best when everyone is out shopping, visiting, or "being seen," even if I must sometimes walk in the street because of the crowd.

Early on Sunday morning the silence inspires reflection on Via Zamboni. The fragments of medieval wall bordering Piazza Verdi blends in comfortably with the graceful sculpted cornice and arch of the adjacent portico.

In the narrow darkness of the tired porticoes in the Jewish Ghetto, their mustiness and the cold smell of "old" call up images of the ancient, medieval city.

The echoes off the stone and brick under the porticoes are especially beautiful when Bologna's church bells serenade my late afternoon excursions.

Sitting in the shade of a portico at a table outside a bar, I read the paper, scour a map or guidebook, or just watch the sky as the sun and clouds jostle to dominate the scene. I sometimes wonder at an ornamental balcony across the way. Who has stood there during the centuries? What have they seen?

I prop myself against a column on the raised sidewalk under the portico of Palazzo Bolognini-Isolani (Via Santo Stefano 18) and watch the world walk or pedal by. I note the symmetry of the Renaissance palazzi on the other side, the curve of their arcades, up and down, up and down, into the distance.

The parade of ocher-toned houses in Via Castiglione looks different every day, depending on the position of the sun. The tall narrow columns and the gentle curve of the arches create lovely images, designs that emerge as shadows alter imperceptibly.

Painted sunny yellow and pumpkin orange, the threadlike passageway of Via Saragozza ambles toward the Meloncello with myriad transformations along the way. Then slices of light cut across the tunnel of 666 stairs as it winds up to the Santuario di San Luca, perched high on Colle della Guardia.

Then too, a walk in the rain really isn't, under Bologna's porticoes.

Bologna Reflections

A sidewalk display of goods under a portico always teases me inside a store. Then I sometimes find myself way back into the bowels of a dark space with a surprisingly large collection of practical house wares and gadgets. Naturally, a little sack of unnecessary acquisitions will probably exit with me.

I am part of the *barista's* day in Via San Vitale, just as he is part of mine. He looks out above his counter as I hurry past and smiles and waves. I am pleased that he recognizes me. I feel part of the neighborhood. The portico makes us all seem close.

Looking up into the nooks and crannies under the porticoes, I find treasures every day—little shrines, a new shade of ocher, a door knocker that catches the sunlight, a store window so beautifully dressed that I can't help but go inside. "Take time and pay attention," I propose. "Com' è bella, la vita—how beautiful!"

Figure 6. Evolution of Porticoes, Via Clavature 14–18

Figure 7. Palazzo Fantuzzi, Via San Vitale 23

Toward Sunrise and the Sea

I like to walk on Via San Vitale at night. The shadows creep and crawl along beside me, while voices and footsteps echo under the arcades. I imagine myself inside a swirling serpent winding its way eastward out of the city, toward the salt marshes of Cervia and the promise of dawn at the Adriatic Sea. Via San Vitale, named after one of Bologna's earliest martyrs, curves gently east from the Piazza di Porta Ravegnana at the foot of the Torri Asinelli and Garisenda. Two ancient gates, the *torresotto* at Piazza Aldrovandi and the thirteenth century porta that opens onto the modern viale punctuate it.

It was a quiet Sunday evening in late March, many years ago, when I took my first walk under the porticoes. For months before my arrival in Bologna, I had looked at the tourist map of the city and tried to imagine life as a resident on Via San Vitale, where I had arranged to rent an apartment while I studied Italian in Bologna. I had dreamed of yellow, pink, and sand-beige castles, of tall towers, and of basilicas with marble facades, chiseled, polished, and intricately inlaid with green, red, and gold. They were images of other Italian cities I had already visited: Firenze, Venezia, Palermo, and Roma. I had not imagined shadowy porticoes and a city of red bricks, where churches often hid from view. That first evening, as the sun was setting and darkness fell heavily under the porticoes, disappointment hung as heavily in my soul as the darkness outside. Via San Vitale seemed so dreary and dusty. I found a public phone to call home, but the traffic noise bouncing off stone that lined the narrow via made it difficult to hear my husband's voice at the other end. I kept thinking, "Tomorrow I will see how beautiful Bologna really is."

The apartment at Via San Vitale 32 became the center of my universe and every day the circle widened while the list of reasons to never leave Bologna multiplied. I have a photograph that captures the view of towers and sky I saw every time I opened the skylight in the bedroom, stood on the bed, and poked my head up through the roof to look out. The evening I snapped the photo, the sun was setting and the bells from San Giacomo Maggiore and other neighborhood churches were gloriously ringing the hour. High above the dark roofs, the black silhouettes of the Torre Asinelli and the steeple of San Bartolomeo were in the company of other tilting towers and needle-thin TV antennas tipping gently to and fro. The sky teemed with billowy clouds as I watched the distant pink center of the heavens transform magically to undulating waves of mauve, then lavender, then every imaginable shade of blue and purple. The photo holds it all for me: the sounds and the colors as the sky deepened into night.

I often drank my morning coffee while gazing out the kitchen window at the ridges of red tile roofs, a hodgepodge of angles, shapes, and tones of Bologna's red. I admired rooftop terrazze strewn with miniature trees and rectangular balconies with potted basil plants and cascading pink geraniums. Strings of flapping sheets and dangling blue jeans usually stretched between adjacent palazzi.

That apartment served as the base for my initial discoveries of Bologna. From my roost there I could see a crenellated wall of Palazzo Orsi (28–30). The Orsi were an important senatorial family of sixteenth century Bologna, and Francesco Morandi, called the Terribilia, the architect of the Archiginnasio, designed the building, which was built between 1549 and 1564. The wall protected the palazzo from the street and hid the courtyard from passersby and even from me, high above, provoking my curiosity. I imagined open space or a garden inside. Entrance to the private palazzo was normally blocked by two portoni on Via San Vitale, but one weekday morning I saw they were open and entered. Inside the first door (30) I was disappointed to find a parking lot paved with river rocks. An elegant porticoed walkway edged it, and hinted at the courtyard's more elegant past. When I entered the other portone (28), my curiosity paid off. Opposite the entrance a stony, gray wall captured my attention and drew me further back. The molded form of a man emerged from it, aslant and rotating, poised to launch an object. He seemed to float suspended over a graceful, oval bowl that also protruded out from the wall. I had found the tranquil courtyard a world away from the bustle of Via San Vitale.

Acquiring life's necessities like bread, coffee, milk, pasta, fruit, and vegetables also pulled me outside into the neighborhood. I practiced Italian as I bought milk and cheese in a *latteria* and chose bread in a *panificio*. I fumbled with the money and the language but met Bolognesi who were patient and tried to understand me. They seemed pleased when I returned to their shops, eager to converse despite my ragged Italian. Little by little, the necessities conquered, I began to notice details of the street and its day-to-day life.

The buildings blend together on Via San Vitale, the particulars of their frontage obscured beneath a practically continuous line of porticoes. Palazzo Fantuzzi (Via San Vitale 23), alone without porticoes, stands out. The structure hulks over the neighborhood although the centuries have smoothed the edges of its gray and rosy pink front. Colossal elephants that bear turreted castles parade across the facade while their little calves trail around the window frames. The pachyderms represent the family's heraldic shield, which perhaps hark back to a former name, Elefantuzzi. The impressive edifice was considered unconventional and spectacular when built on behalf of the Bolognese senator

Bologna Reflections

Francesco Fantuzzi during the first half of the sixteenth century. Formigine has been identified as one of its architects. The senator wanted to dazzle us with his massive palazzo and he does.

From the corner of Via Caldarese it is possible to imagine the Fantuzzi elephants on a march, their heavy limbs pounding the timeworn stones of Via San Vitale. The image spills over into the surrounding architecture so that the tremendous gold and grimy pink legs of the porticoes also march ponderously toward the ancient porta as the street curves east beyond view.

I first noticed the church of SS. Vitale and Agricola in Arena (Via San Vitale 50) late one afternoon when the open door allowed me a glimpse inside. I had missed it for weeks. Because a ceremony was underway that day, I decided to return later to explore the inner regions. Meanwhile I lingered to read the memorial to Lucio de' Liuzzi, a professor at the early medical school, embedded in the russet wall to the left of the church's entrance. In 1318 his nephew Mondino commissioned Rosso da Parma to create the monument. Mondino was the first in medical history, in 1315, to teach anatomy and describe the parts of the body based on dissection of human cadavers. The sarcophagus in the wall under the portico actually holds the remains of both de' Liuzzi men.

Although the church is small, the interior is unexpectedly striking. A giant canvas hangs over the main altar, its brilliant gold frame illuminating the darkness. The painting by Luigi Busi (1874) depicts the double martyrdom of the slave Vitale and his master Agricola in a Roman arena around 303–305 AD. Like other Christians they were executed during the reign of Emperor Diocletian. Sant'Ambrogio and San Petronio, protectors of the medieval city, consecrated the first church at this site to the early martyrs in 430 AD. Evidence suggests that ruins of the arena may be underneath the crypt. At that time this part of the bustling modern city was well outside the inhabited area of Roman Bononia and would have been surrounded by trees and cultivated fields.

32

My first visit to what is perhaps the oldest crypt in Bologna risked turning into an unsettling adventure. From the darkness of the church above, I descended into the even dimmer Romanesque chamber. I sat in the silence, noticing its three naves and apse, alone but for the relics of the two martyrs. The dark, cave-like space, damp and bare, had been built in the twelfth century of coarse materials, primarily brick and stone, clearly the ruins of other, more ancient structures. Pillars of varying sizes and shapes had been adapted to fit the space. The plain capitals exhibited modest workmanship. Big sheets of stone, fragments of six-sided marble slabs, and Roman bricks formed the floor that in ancient times had been at street level. The layers of history represented there, together with the roughness of the materials and simplicity of the little space, evoked in me a sense of the mystery and severity of the past.

Engrossed in my thoughts, I suddenly heard clanking and the scrape of metal on stone. I woke up from my reverie and realized that someone was locking the gate with me inside! I yelled "Sono qui, nella cripta! Please let me out!" The old gentleman held the gate open as I ran up the stairs, a bit shaken. He mumbled something about informing him the next time *before* I enter silently and sit down there so quietly. I will!

The pretty eighteenth century house in Via San Vitale (56) was where Cornelia Rossi Martinetti received Lord Byron; Louis, King of Bavaria; and other literati of her time. It was designed by her husband, architect Giovanni Battista Martinetti, and stands next to the Torresotto di Via San Vitale, one of the remaining city gates of the Cerchia del Mille. While a whimsical weathervane whips about energetically in the wind on the tower's cap, the gate's arch bows over the width of the narrow street like a horse's saddle, the vaulted opening slightly askew from carrying the weight of the centuries on its back. Remnants of the ancient brick wall are visible inside the street level store at Via San Vitale 54/H and bordering the sidewalk.

Bologna Reflections

To the right of the *torresotto*, Piazza Aldrovandi opens up between Via San Vitale and Strada Maggiore. At one time the piazza was part of the ancient moat outside the Cerchia del Mille. As the piazza evolved, river stones paved what became known as the *Salegata* (paved with river stones) di Strada Maggiore. One by one merchants began to set up stalls in this area to sell their wares to the people in the neighborhood who lived a distance from the center of the city. Over the years, the stands loaded with fruit and vegetables that edge up to the porticoed sidewalk on the east side of the piazza have become part of my day-to-day life. Friendly bars and small shops across from the stalls open up under the portico. They sell everything from antique books to fresh bread and salami. In spirit and character the piazza has always resembled a medieval market with *bancarelle* (stalls or carts) and cloth awnings or tents. The most recent renovation tried to keep that spirit alive, although the constant vehicular traffic makes it seem more a busy street than a bustling piazza.

Sometimes I set out on Via San Vitale and decide to deviate left or right on one of the small streets crossing it on either side. Little houses, painted various shades of gold and rusty ocher, line Via dell'Unione, Via Apollonia, and Via San Leonardo. Many of them boast *sporti* (bulges) that overhang the narrow passage like shelves and create additional house space. A fourteenth century house at Via Begatto 17 was once the Orphanage of San Leonardo. The heads of the carved angels that trim the doorway are reminiscent of the children who lived there. The low, wooden portico, the dirty brown bricks, the windows with pointed arches, and the dank smell emanating from within suggest an ancient world that reluctantly divulges the secrets locked inside.

I like to cross from Via San Vitale to Strada Maggiore on Via Broccaindosso, a street that smells of dampness. Even when the sun is shining, it is usually dark under the porticoes of the typical fifteenth century working class houses lining the street whose name has always puzzled me. Bolognesi

34

offer a number of explanations. One person I questioned believes that it refers to *brocca*, the Italian word for a large vase with handles used in the past to hold water and other liquids, and *indosso*, conjuring up an image of people carrying the jug of water on their heads. In the Bolognese dialect *brocca* means "tree branch." Once upon a time, some say, there was a tree on the street (none today) whose branches were so low that they would hit passersby on their head (*addosso*) as they walked by. Other clarifications exist as well and make for good conversation over dinner in one of the street's many trattorie.

At L'Aura 71/C Laura can usually be found hunched over her worktable, painting ceramic objects in majolica style. She specializes in recreating ancient patterns but will also fashion new designs. Laura painstakingly decorates small covered boxes, plates, and an assortment of vases, bells, tiles and other functional and ornamental objects. She studies ancient manuscripts, paintings, and historic texts to research her creations. When I visit, she always stops to talk about her family, work, and Bologna. The lid of my own small covered dish at home recalls a pavement tile from the Capella Vaselli in the basilica of San Petronio. Its rich royal blue and white flowery design, with russet fans that look like peacock tails, always transports me back to Bologna whenever I glance at it in its position of honor on my coffee table in San Francisco. And I think of Laura who generously shares her knowledge of Bologna's ancient past with me.

Once I began my adventure in earnest so many years ago, I fell in love with Bologna. The images I have carried with me since that first evening as I stood under the portico at the red phone booth next to the newspaper stand caught fire and have inspired any number of discoveries. My history now merges with that of the city. The shadows that creep and crawl along beside me and the voices and footsteps that echo under the arcades are really my own memories welcoming me home again, to Bologna.

Bologna Reflections

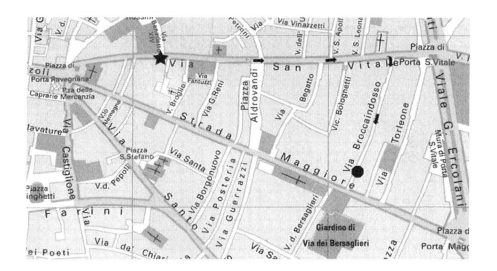

Map for *Toward Sunrise and the Sea*

Figure 8. Street Study

Neighborhoods

Figure 9. Relaxing in Piazza Maggiore

Time and Again in Piazza Maggiore

L ate afternoon in Piazza Maggiore is magic. Streaks and splashes of light bathe the earthy ocher and terracotta stones of the ancient edifices that have circumscribed the space for centuries. The setting sun pierces the voluminous cloud mountains, decorating the moving sky with shafts of light that play across the basilica of the city's patron, San Petronio, and the other palazzi. The piazza shimmers. The spell is cast again.

The insistent ringing of the clock tower marks the five o'clock hour and I say to myself blissfully, "Bologna—I'm back!" Life buzzes on and around the *crescentone*, the large center pancake of a stage in the middle of the square, the heart of the city.

Piazza Maggiore is usually full of people at this time of day. They sit at little round, linen-draped tables and outside the bars that line the grand space, eating a gelato or drinking an aperitif. They occupy the wide steps of the basilica of San Petronio or step inside to say a quick prayer before the doors are locked for the evening. They gather in helter-skelter discussion groups. They push their children in elegant strollers or watch them chase the pigeons or a big red ball. They ride their bicycles on the way to somewhere, or stop and lean on them, relaxed, during a friendly conversation. They walk arm in arm together, just to stroll, to get some air, to be together.

Bologna Reflections

Sometimes I pretend to be a tourist when I return. I stand in the middle and soak in the harmony. I focus on certain small aspects of each edifice as I turn around in place, dodging the pigeons and the bustling people. Soft pink, rose and mauve, a smattering of gray and white, are as comfortable as the rhythm of arches and porticoes lining the space, as the uniform height of the buildings. The afternoon light fuses and diffuses, shadows and hides.

The *Madonna di Piazza* by Nicolò dell'Arca (1478) always grabs my attention. Positioned between the two windows to the left of the massive portone of the Palazzo Comunale, the seat of city government, the *Madonna di Piazza* commemorates the victory of Bologna over the troops of the Visconti family of Milan, who, at the time of the Bentivoglio, attempted to take over the city. As I move toward the building the young Madonna watches me from above. Everything about her is soft and rosy thanks to the terracotta. She holds up her child as if to say, "Look, look at my baby. Isn't he beautiful?" A glance around the piazza reveals many of today's young Bolognese mothers strolling proudly through the square with their own babies. Here the past and the present merge.

Most guided tours begin in Piazza Maggiore and rightly so. The palazzi and the basilica, symbols of the city's civil, economic, and religious power, speak of history. In 1200 Bologna, proud and rich, became an autonomous *Comune*, subject to neither papal nor imperial rule, and turned its attention to the construction of public buildings and spaces in the next century. The construction of what we today call Piazza Maggiore and of the monumental basilica was begun within the next century. A lively marketplace, as well as urgent town meetings, hangings, and civic and religious celebrations drew citizens to the new center of city life.

It took centuries for Piazza Maggiore to arrive at its present look, flanked on the eastern side by Palazzo dei Banchi, to the south by the basilica of

San Petronio and Palazzo dei Notai, on the western side by Palazzo Comunale, and to the north by Palazzo del Podestà and its complex of buildings. Harmony and beauty characterize the space.

Some things never seem to change in the piazza. Life beats strongly, as any healthy heart does. In 1222 St. Francis of Assisi preached. Napoleon came and went more than once in the nineteenth century. A woman named Gentile Cimieri, considered the most powerful Bolognese witch ever, was accused of witchcraft by the inquisitor of San Domenico in 1498, found guilty by a jury of Doctors of Canon Law in the basilica of San Petronio, and burned at the stake in Piazza Maggiore. A most theatrical event for the citizens, and legend says that not even her ash remains could be detected when the fire had subsided.

Today crowds gather to stage protests or to party, people chat quietly while others sit, pensive, alone. Groups of men here and there discuss politics and soccer. Crowds of pigeons join the gathering, to scavenge bits of food, teasing everyone with swoops above our heads and tangling our steps with quick, unanticipated landings. Happy children set aside their tricycles to chase them under the watchful eyes of parents or grandparents.

Someone is always standing around Nettuno's Fountain, waiting for a friend—or a stranger. On Sunday afternoons, the muscular Beppe Maniglia, dressed from head to foot in sleek black leather, tosses back his long, light brown hair and plays his guitar fervently. The pounding, electronic music blasts from his unique psychedelic amplifier-motorcycle and echoes off the walls of the stone palazzi in Piazza del Nettuno. Crowds of people gather around him to keep time and pass time, even listening sometimes, to Beppe's predications on life and the importance of being kind to one other.

There are always new events, too. One Sunday morning a parade of vintage military vehicles, and their equally vintage drivers, entered the city to commemorate the entry of Allied troops into Bologna at the end of World War II. They parked in the square, where I meandered and enjoyed the excitement of Bolognese grandmas and grandpas showing them off to their grandchildren, explaining that day and how it changed their lives. I could hardly get through Piazza Maggiore one afternoon because a throng of people from all over the world were waiting patiently for Pope John Paul II to emerge from under the canopy on a stage constructed in front of the basilica.

Sometimes on a weekday morning I hurry straight across the piazza. Then it's a place on the way to somewhere else: to work, the market, to school or to a doctor's appointment.

Then, late at night when the piazza is quiet and nearly empty, I can hear the splash of the fountain and the echo of footsteps and voices under the porticoes. I watch the lights play against the darkness, contemplating the shadows of the past and the promise of the present and future.

Poking Around the Piazza

Flocks of parading pigeons push and peck,

Favoring the crescentone, the broad pink and

Gray stone slab of Bologna's center stage.

All day they fight for space in Piazza Maggiore—

The feet, the wheels of prams and trikes.

Yikes. Watch out!

They pick up crumbs, whatever.

Clean the place? No.

Try to interact? Well—

Look, the bright, beautiful children

With chips or sweets—ready to snag?

There it dropped. Wing right over.

Push right in. Grab it. Quick.

There it's done. What fun.

The pigeons.

Then WH-O-O-S-S-S-H!

The troops take flight.

In an instant they are up, up

Just high enough to

Skim my ducking head.

A storm . . . around, around, one

Colossal swoop, together, they wheel around

Clockwise, together . . . a roar of motion . . .

Then suddenly stop, alight, there.

It's over. Back to flocks of

Parading pigeons poking

Around the piazza.

Piazza Maggiore.

Bologna.

Figure 10. Basilica of San Petronio, Facade

A Closer Look At Piazza Maggiore

The Basilica of San Petronio

In 1388 the General Council of the Six Hundred of the People, Bologna's governing body, decreed that the basilica of San Petronio be built to honor Bologna's patron saint. The foundation stone was put down on June 7, 1390. Petronio, the city's eighth bishop from 431–450 AD, not only strengthened Roman Catholicism in Bologna but also, thanks to his administrative talent and power, made an important contribution to political stability.

The architect Antonio di Vincenzo was engaged to design the basilica, which the Bolognese intended to be the largest church in Christendom. For centuries work went forward, until finally, in 1659, the apse was finished. The basilica was never completely finished, due largely to changes in the city's political and economic fortunes.

The Italian Gothic facade of the temple is brazenly incomplete. The top portion is bare brickwork, while the lower is lined with elegant decorations in precious white and pink marble. Lunettes depicting the *Resurrection of Christ* (Alfonso Lombardi) and the *Burial of Christ* (Amico Aspertini and his assistants) sit above the left and right entrances. The great sculptor from Siena, Jacobo della Quercia, decorated the frame of the main entrance with an early Renaissance masterpiece. Each square in bas-relief recounts an episode from the narratives of the *Fall of Man* and the *Redemption*. The lunette above the great door holds statues of the Madonna with Christ Child, Sant'Ambrogio, and San Petronio, with the walled city in his hands.

The hollow silence echoing inside the huge interior affords a moment's respite from the activity unfolding in the busy piazza. The official city colors of red and white dominate. In almost every corner or chapel an arresting sculpture, fresco, or detail competes for attention. The astronomer Domenico Cassini's meridian slices across the floor from the southeast toward the north, and a small eyehole in the ceiling above allows a stream of light to break through and signal the date at the appropriate point on the floor's meridian. Four protective crosses, said to have been set at the four corners of the city by Saints Ambrogio and Petronio, evoke distant times.

~

Palazzo dei Notai

The Palazzo dei Notai stands to the right of the basilica in the piazza. The guildhall's prominent position testifies to the power that the Corporation of the Notaries wielded in medieval Bologna. The city's notaries, responsible for drawing up official contracts between the parties involved in any purchase or loan, managed to keep busy in this city where commerce flourished and merchants thrived. The guild and its individual members often wielded significant political power in the city as well.

The Corporation of the Notaries commissioned their Palazzo de' Notai in 1381. In the early twentieth century, Alfonso Rubbiani, a fervent adherent of the Neo-Gothic style, to whose judgment a significant program of urban renewal was entrusted by the city, undertook the restoration of the building. Some complain that his changes were too drastic because they favored those architectural elements that created a romantic medieval effect, instead of preserving the embellishments added after the Middle Ages.

~

Palazzo Comunale

The name Palazzo Comunale refers to the cluster of buildings on the west side of Piazza Maggiore where today's city government is headquartered. The original structures belonged to the family of Accursio, a Bolognese scholar who taught law at the ancient university. In 1284 the palazzo was sold to the Comune and became the city granary. The porticoed section of the building, an example of Gothic style, dates back to 1287 and the clock tower to 1444. At one time it boasted a complex mechanical clock with moving statues. Today's simpler one dates to the eighteenth century.

In the fifteenth century Palazzo d'Accursio was extended, joining Renaissance elements to the existing Gothic ones. The addition became the residence of the executive magistrates and later of the papal legate. The whole complex was a walled fortress with battlements and towers in the fourteenth century, because the volatile political situation and factional wars called for protective measures. At the base of the complex, near the center of the two buildings facing onto Piazza Maggiore, it is possible to see where Bolognese measurements were carved into Istrian stone. The vendors and artisans used this "ruler" in their negotiations when the piazza hosted the city market. Two sculpted eagles of red marble from Verona rest under the splendid Renaissance window that marks the beginning of Piazza del Nettuno. The one on the left is thought to be the work of Michelangelo.

It would be difficult to miss the monumental bronze statue of Pope Gregory XIII (Alessandro Menganti), the notable Bolognese who reformed the Julian calendar in 1582. It sits above the huge central entrance to the palazzo. I enter the courtyard under his watchful eye and walk across it. There is an elevator, but I prefer the graceful stairway, attributed to Bramante and said to have been built to accommodate the gait of horses. In 1530 Charles V moved under canopies from Palazzo Accursio to the basilica of San Petronio where Pope Clement VII crowned him Holy Roman Emperor. I wonder if he and his retinue on horseback took advantage of the staircase on their way to the momentous event.

Palazzo Comunale boasts many elegant rooms and two museums on the second floor, as well as other hidden treasures. The Sala d'Ercole (Hercules' Hall) on the first floor takes its name from the giant statue of the demi-god located there. The space is home to a fresco by Francesco Francia, the *Madonna del terremoto* (*Madonna of the Earthquake*, 1505), which was commissioned to celebrate the city's survival after a terrible earthquake. The image of the fifteenth century city, resting under the protective gaze of the Madonna and Child, shows how the city walls closed everything in, protecting Bologna from the menacing perils of the time.

As I study the image, I try to guess where Francesco Francia might have stood to sketch this view of medieval Bologna. On many a clear day from one of the higher hills in Villa Ghigi, I have seen the same sweet contours of rolling earth, the same grand facade of the Aula Magna of the University, once
50

the church of Santa Lucia. Bologna's towers are in the fresco, not only the famous Asinelli and Garisenda, but a hundred others that were destroyed long ago. From the hill I have not only seen the ancient towers and church cupolas that remain, but also the towers of the modern skyscrapers of the convention center or Fiera District, which help make Bologna one of modern Europe's important commercial centers. The fresco also shows the basilica of San Francesco, with its flying buttresses and bell towers that jut up higher than anything in the neighborhood. From my perch on the hill, the basilica looked identical to the artist's depiction. The elegant gates of Bologna's southern city wall, distinguishable still from the hill in the park, are also visible in the painting. I see Porta Saragozza and Porta Castiglione, too, and imagine the medieval travelers who wended their way on dangerous roads toward the walled city.

When I leave Sala d'Ercole I turn right and proceed down the hall until I reach another large painting on the left that depicts Irnerio, the renowned scholar and teacher of secular Roman law, another of Bologna's heroes. Irnerio is thought to be responsible for Justinian's set of laws arriving in Bologna from Ravenna, the seat of the Eastern Roman Empire, where they had ended up after the fall of Rome and the West. The painting shows him studying and explaining the Justinian code as troops behind him go off to war. In the distance, masses of people flaunt the red and white banners of the proud city against a backdrop of soft green fields and Bologna off in the distance, her red brick towers sticking up into the bright blue sky. I leave Irnerio, young, solitary, hard at work, and climb to the next floor.

After Rome Bologna was the most important city in the Papal States. The chapel and apartments on this floor of the palazzo were used by the papal legate, the official representative of the Pope and the governor of the city. From the balcony at the end of the magnificent Sala Farnese, as this room is known, I look out over Piazza Maggiore and at the zigzagging red roofs of the surrounding buildings. Bologna has long been known as the Città Rossa, once because of the red bricks and tiles that built her edifices and for much of the second half of the twentieth century because of her modern political history as a stronghold of the Italian Communist party.

The city's main library has been housed in the Sala Borsa, originally the stable for the papal legate's quarters, since December 2001. The ruins of the ancient city are visible through a Plexiglas floor in the library's stunning Piazza Coperta. On a tour of the excavations, one can see at close hand elements of Roman Bononia: the wall of its ancient basilica and the imprint of wheel-tracks on stony, street pavement from the age of Augustus. It is thrilling to distinguish them, along with the remains of medieval streets and structures, and the underpinnings of the colossal, cruciform tub of the Orto dei Semplici (Garden of Medicinal Herbs), which was cultivated here from the sixteenth to the eighteenth centuries. The building's current name derives from its history as a commodities trading center in the nineteenth century, even though Bologna's first basketball court was a later metamorphosis in the 1960s.

~

Palazzo del Podestà

The Palatium Vetus (old palace), now known as Palazzo del Podestà, fills the north side of the square across from the basilica of San Petronio. It was built in the early thirteenth century to house the city's seat of power and its tribunal. The Renaissance facade was added in 1484 during the *signoria* (rule) of Giovanni II Bentivoglio.

The nucleus of buildings, which includes Palazzo del Podestà, Palazzo Re Enzo, and the Palazzo del Capitano del Popolo, is the oldest in the piazza. The Torre dell'Arengo rises up over its roof. Beginning in 1456 the *campana grossa*, the tower's big bell, called the citizens to meet in the square and warned them of approaching danger.

Above the arches of the porticoes there was once a *ringhiera*, a railing or banister, from which the authorities informed the public of government decisions and criminal sentences. Executions occasionally took place right there when they threw the condemned over the edge of the building with the rope around his neck.

The huge room on the top level of the palazzo has served a variety of purposes over the centuries. It was originally constructed to house the tribunal and the offices of the city government. Later it was used for the conclave of cardinals that elected the antipope Giovanni XXIII during the Roman Catholic Church's Great Schism (1378–1418). At another point in time it was even restructured for theatrical performances. Now the space accommodates a variety of exhibits and gatherings.

Under the Voltone del Podestà, the vaulted space where four alleyways coincide under the Palazzo del Podestà, it is usually dark, silent, damp, and musty. For centuries, however, it was one of the busiest places in the city. Vendors, their clients, mendicant monks, troublemakers, the homeless and hungry, and even the important notaries exercised their respective trades underneath it. In 1525 statues of the four protector saints of Bologna—San Petronio, San Domenico, San Francesco d'Assisi, and San Procolo—were placed at the four corners of the *voltone*. It is said that if one stands facing the wall and whispers into one of the vault's four corners, someone standing in the opposite corner one will hear every word. Try it—it works!

Palazzo dei Banchi

The broad Palazzo dei Banchi on the east side of the piazza is not really a palazzo, but a facade. The architect Jacopo Barozzi, better known as Vignola, was commissioned in the sixteenth century to give this side of the piazza the same dignity as the other three. By hiding the existing old houses behind a facade, he created the illusion of a grand palazzo yet preserved access to the modest shops on Via Clavature and Via Pescherie Vecchie.

Moneychangers and bankers sitting at their small desks, or *banchi*, once transacted deals in this area close to the market, giving the gigantic false front its name. Its rhythmic arcades supported by Corinthian pilasters and two tiers of windows complement the other important buildings on the square.

Figure 11. Studies of San Sepolcro and Porta San Donato

Bologna's City Walls

The city walls that have circumscribed Bologna over the centuries, like protective arms that embrace her, still give a visual structure to the recounting of her history. They were built during the Middle Ages to guard against the danger of threatening barbarians, imperial armies, brigands, and whatever fantastic monster a world of magic and alchemy could imagine.

The oldest circle of walls, called the Cerchia di Selenite, were built between the third or fourth and the seventh centuries. They were constructed to protect the southeastern part of the Roman city from the barbarians. Created with blocks of selenite (gypsum) from Monte Donato, a hill south of Bologna, they encircled an area roughly one-third the size of the Imperial Roman city of Bononia. From 728–729 AD the Addizione Longobarda attached a semicircle of fortified territory, more or less the Piazza di Porta Ravegnana, to that already guarded by the Wall of Selenite. The gates of the Cerchia di Selenite were Porta San Pietro (Piero), Porta San Procolo (Procola), Porta Stiera, and Porta Ravennate (Ravegnana). The wall was about 26.25 feet high and enclosed an area of approximately 45 acres.

The second set of walls from the period of the independent Comune expanded the city outward to include little outlying towns. It was called the Cerchia dei Torresotti, for its characteristic towered gates that allowed traffic to pass underneath, or del Mille, for the date of its construction beginning in the year 1000 AD. The purpose of the expanded set of walls was to protect the city from the advancing army of Emperor Frederick Barbarossa, who is said to have battered down much of the earlier one. Construction began in 1176 and finished in 1192. It had sixteen gates or outlooks and two smaller secondary ones. The brick crenellated walls were roughly 26 feet high and had a perimeter of nearly 2.5 miles that encircled an area of about 247 acres. The Torresotto di San Vitale, which is about 65 feet high, is an existing example of one of its gates.

In 1226, because of the threatening army of Emperor Frederick II, the Comune first constructed the third set of city walls in wood with gates raised in brick. The wall itself was eventually rebuilt in brick a century later, beginning in 1337. The perimeter was over 4 miles long and its height 29 feet. Besides the twelve gates (ten are still standing) numerous towers and *baraccani* (barracks) augmented the defensive structure.

Figure 12. Church of Santa Maria della Vita, Mary Magdalene

The Marys Weeping

S hrieks of horror and lamentation—the dramatic passion of Mary Magdalene grips me as I approach the seven life-size terracotta shapes in the corner chapel of the church of Santa Maria della Vita (Via Clavature 10). The heavy clothing of Mary Magdalene whips out behind her solid, muscular body that is impelled by grief. Veil, shawl, and gown cannot counter the violent, forward impulse. Her eyes incline down toward the dead Christ. Her left leg lunges ahead, suspended in motion. Piercing screams issue from her mouth, opened past possibility. Disbelief and horror stab her heart beyond endurance. Like a storm, she cannot be contained. Her passion and pain explode; the figure personifies the howl of pain.

The voluptuous torso under heavy robes, the circles of her full breasts, and the striding strong legs breathe physicality and humanness into the terracotta statue, part of the group called *Le Marie Piangenti sul Cristo Morto* (*The Weeping Marys Seeing the Dead Christ*, 1463) by Nicolò dell'Arca. Mary Magdalene's slender face is refined, her nose, long and thin, her hair modestly covered with a veil soaring out behind her. Both arms are bent back so that the cricks of each elbow catch the flowing garments. Her left hand is palm forward, fully opened, incredulous. The rigid, bent fingers of her right hand would grab, if they could, another hand, someone, to ease the pain.

Bologna Reflections

To Mary Magdalene's right, Mary Cleofe is also moving forward violently, but the position of her hands says, "I cannot look." She would like to shield her eyes from the horror, but they are opened wide, full of fear. Her body swerves toward the right as she runs and stops short of the Christ stretched out below. Her gown flows to the right, following the curve of her body. The cloth of her headpiece's flaps fly out in all directions, reflecting the sudden stop; the deep creases in her cheeks accentuate the wailing mouth. She tries to say something, his name, perhaps. She was his aunt, wife of the brother of Christ's mother.

John, the Beloved Apostle, stands silently immobile beside her. Chin rests on his right hand, while his left arm and hand lay under his cloak, supporting the right elbow. His narrow face, framed by softly curling, chin-length hair, holds back pain and sorrow. He would like to turn away, pull the cloak that he already uses to shield his right side, up over his eyes. Then he might permit the tears to escape freely.

Mary, Jesus' mother, stands to John's right. Her shoulders are raised, her folded hands press up close to her abdomen. Her mouth is open but nothing escapes. She only inhales. She will never exhale, releasing the sorrow and pain. The wrinkled forehead, raised eyebrows, closed eyes, and fleshy cheeks communicate maturity. Her heavy clothing hangs motionless, just as the grief-filled moment hangs suspended in eternity.

Mary Salome, the mother of John the Evangelist, cringes next to Christ's mother. From her open mouth comes a deep, animal-like moan, emitted from the center of her being. Her crouched position, with flexed, tense hands on upper legs, keeps her planted in place. Her substantial robes do not move. The horror and disbelief cry out from her soul as her knees fold toward the floor.

Joseph of Arimathea looks out, not down at the Christ figure like the others. He holds a short hammer in his right hand. A pair of long-handled pliers hangs on his belt, the claw-like talons slightly open. His role is a practical one as he kneels down at the head of Christ. Pilate has granted him custody of the Savior's body, which he will place in his own sepulcher. The Sabbath is quickly approaching and, according to the law, his duty must be carried out with haste. Joseph wears a heavy tunic with precise tucks that fall neatly over his hefty chest, ample abdomen, and wide waist. He is a decisive man, used to controlling the situation. His hat, mustache, and neatly trimmed, curly beard frame a serious face.

Christ, the central figure, lies on a body-length plank covered with a scallop-edged linen cloth. His head rests on a tasseled pillow, caught in peaceful sleep. His arms rest on the torso, while hands cross his pelvis, which is covered by a light, gauzy cloth. The lightness, silence, and serenity of the figure forms the eye of the storm around which the action and emotion of the group erupt.

The figures represent the group of loved ones that visits the sepulcher and to whom Christ appears after his death. Each gospel narrates the events differently, and the persons present are not always the same in each account. However, Mary Magdalene, the most important female disciple of Christ, does play a significant role in each one. This sort of statuary group, known as a *compianto* (mourning) is found throughout Italy and is thought to be a later manifestation of the medieval mystery play or dramatic Easter matins services played out at convents and monasteries throughout Europe. The action and emotion of the depiction was intended to move the faithful to deep grief.

Other versions exist in Bologna, *Il Compianto su Cristo Morto* (*Mourning Over the Dead Christ*) by Alfonso Lombardi (1497–1537), in the cathedral of San Pietro in Via dell'Indipendenza 7, and *The Pietà* by Vincenzo Onofri (sixteenth century) in the basilica of San Petronio, Piazza Maggiore.

Bologna Reflections

Terracotta was the characteristic medium for the *compianti* in Bologna because the region lacked marble and other hard stone normally used by sculptors. The material's softness permitted the artists to create powerful dramatic expression and exquisite detail. A meaningful portrait of an individual could emerge from the clay, his precise physical characteristics and richly textured garments. These figures of Nicolò dell'Arca attest to that eloquence. Originally painted, they are now left in their natural rosy terracotta simplicity.

I leave the hollow, dark silence of the church of Santa Maria della Vita, the memory of Mary Magdalene's shriek still echoing, the images and sounds inside receding. Meanwhile, the boisterous life outside in the Quadrilatero welcomes me back to today.

Figure 13. *The Weeping Marys Seeing the Dead Christ*

Figure 14. Shopping in Via Pescherie Vecchie

In the Quadrilatero—A Delicious Mix

I f I could stand forever at one corner in Bologna, I would choose Via Pescherie Vecchie where it meets Via Drapperie. The narrow street escapes east from Piazza Maggiore, while the curves and wide windows of an elegant, apricot palazzo form a backdrop to today's market that hugs the edges. The market has evolved in this neighborhood for centuries. The unbroken line of little gingery, gold, and red houses on the left and the vibrant colors of fruit and vegetables on the right light up Bologna's grayest day: red and yellow peppers, shiny purple eggplant, blood oranges from Sicilia, and burgundy radicchio from the Veneto.

Visions of white truffles, pistachios, walnuts, chestnuts, porcini mushrooms, greens of every design and shade, gold squash, green squash, broccoli, fennel, peppers in a myriad of shapes and colors, and seasonal flowers color the scene universally bright. The smells of the neighborhood assault me: roasting chicken on a spit or baking bread, the perfume of hanging prosciutto crudo, ovals of mortadella Bolognese, towers of pungent cheeses, and mounds of fresh tagliatelle and tortelloni.

The barrage of images forces me to stop, regardless of the destination, and consider options for my next meal. I look forward to the Saturday morning ritual of joining the festa. Venders and clients negotiate deals and chatter about the state of health, family, weather, or economy. Miniscule bars overflow with the young, old, foreign, and hometown. Lines of clients spill onto the street from out of the fish stalls and bakeries. Babies in strollers pushed by young parents or strutting *nonne* (grandmothers) navigate the crowd. Tourists and immigrants speaking Japanese, German, Chinese, Spanish, Tagalog, English, and American blend with Italian and its dialect-cousins from north and south, east and west. The local Bolognese vernacular punctuates the hullabaloo that explodes in the crisscross of streets.

The sale of fish and seafood is not confined to Via Pescherie Vecchie, as one would expect. Fresh seafood may also be purchased on Via Drapperie where merchants once sold fabric and carpets. In fact, the fish stalls have often been moved from one place to another over the centuries because of the unpleasant smells associated with them.

This neighborhood, the oldest part of the city, where a delicious mix of ancient Rome, the Middle Ages, and modern Bologna converge, is known as the Quadrilatero. The narrow, regular, checkerboard streets without porticoes reflect the area's origin as a Roman market and give the zone its name: a rectangle delimited by Via Rizzoli, Via Castiglione, Via Farini, and Via dell'Archiginnasio. Given today's still active market scene, it's not difficult to imagine the drama that has unfolded throughout the course of its history. The street designations derive primarily from the Middle Ages and identify the artisans and merchants who sometimes still inhabit them. Via Clavature (locks) was the street of lock and key makers. Other metalworkers would have populated Via Orefici (goldsmiths) and Via Spadari (sword makers). Merchants of foodstuffs would have been found on Via Pescherie Vecchie (old fishmongers) and Via Caprarie (goats), while Via Drapperie (textiles) and Via Calzolerie (shoes) would have been the home of those trades. Early on, venders sold fruit and vegetables from stalls in Piazza Maggiore. Then, in the nineteenth century, the Mercato Coperto (Via Pescherie Vecchie 16) opened and they moved here.

The immediate neighborhood harbors surprises in every nook and cranny. The historic Osteria del Sole is at Via Ranocchi 1. Open since 1465, it is one of the few remaining osterie from ancient Bologna. Today no food is served, so students, shopkeepers on break, old-timers, and clued-in tourists bring their own snacks to accompany the wine and sit at one of the long tables to chat and relax in the late afternoon, enjoying the centuries old Bolognese tradition of meeting at the favorite local osteria.

During the Middle Ages Via Clavature was Bologna's main street. Day-to-day life often included activities of the guilds, which had their headquarters in the quarter, and the shopping and bartering that evolved in the markets. Important processions, like that of Charles V when he was crowned emperor in Bologna in 1530, took a turn here, while the city's first Zecca (mint) operated in Via Clavature in the late 1500s. Nowadays windows of fashion boutiques, glittering jewelry stores, and bakeries, with their tempting fresh bread and cookies, keep me from rushing by.

In the tranquility of the early afternoon, I soak in the shades of Bologna's colors while strolling in the neighborhood—from mustard and gold to rust and rosy red. Shadows cross my path and the sunlight plays off the houses leaning one against the other. Palazzo Schiavina (Via Clavature 16–18) has its origins in the 1200s and is a good place to study the evolution of Bologna's porticoes.

What has changed over the centuries? The market atmosphere? No. The level of hygiene? Yes. The fish sellers and butchers used to throw their garbage into the passing Torrente Aposa. Needless-to-say, the quarter reeked with an unpleasant stench until the waterway was covered over sometime after the seventeenth century.

Wind whips through as I walk under the high, broad portico of the old Via della Morte, now known as Via dei Musei because the Museo Civico (Civic Museum) is housed in what was once the Ospedale della Morte. A bar and lively clubs bring the quiet corner to life, while the display window of the Nanni bookstore shows titles that represent centuries of Bologna's past. At the end of Via dei Musei where it meets Via Toschi, I look out at a stack of houses, the layers of their red tile roofs turned brown with age. Rectangular windows with dull green shutters resemble eyes looking out over the busy shoppers, and smoke stacks tip up toward the sky.

Where Via Marchesana meets Via Foscherari, pieces of the arch that once belonged to the Foscherari family's house are incorporated into the modern architecture. A dark, damp archway creates a shadowy passageway to Via de' Toschi: a perfect spot for secret assignations between lovers and enemies alike, for anyone who seeks the cover of nighttime shadows.

In another corner of the Quadrilatero, where the Palazzo dell'Archiginnasio now stands, the first official brothel of the city prospered during the earliest days of the university. The students looking for lessons in love and the women ready to accommodate them found each other easily in the Osteria della Scimmia, closed down in 1490 because of its notorious reputation. The bordello complex of the Corte dei Bulgari once had houses interspersed from today's Via Farini to the Vicolo della Scimmia (Little Street of the Monkey), a narrow jig-jaggy lane (now Via Massei) back behind the Palazzo dell' Archiginnasio, which gave that first famous house its name.

Piazza del Pavaglione was an early designation for Piazza Galvani. Today's portico is said to echo the huge tent (*pavaglione*) that covered the booths of the venders of the silkworm *bozzoli* or *bachi* (cocoons). I imagine their insistent voices bouncing off the vault walls, as if they were still arguing their transactions. The cocoons were weighed and paid for just on the other side of the arch, in the Pavaglioncino, and I picture huge baskets on the backs of sweating laborers. The shouts and movements of the silk traders joined those of the bankers and other merchants in the Quadrilatero's busy streets, as they still do today.

Bologna Reflections

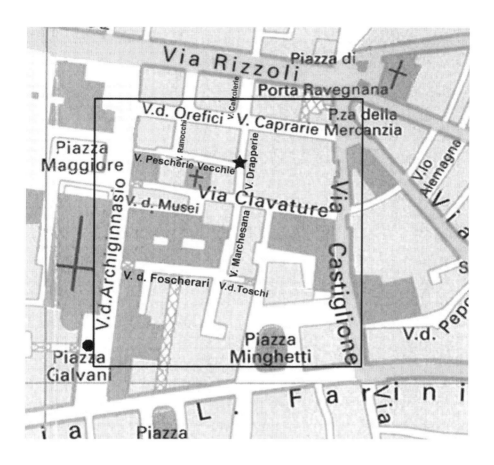

Map for *In the Quadrilatero—A Delicious Mix*

Figure 15. Neptune's Fountain

Seduction

ost Bolognesi were home relaxing at three on a clear spring afternoon, but bands of pecking pigeons crowded me as I crossed the grand piazza toward his place in the center of the smaller one. He stood like a giant above the few people scurrying here and there in Piazza Maggiore and Piazza del Nettuno. I was drawn like a magnet to his unabashed maleness. Head turned, he glanced down, eyes following the curve of his extended left arm, hand reaching out in welcome. His broad, powerful, bronze shoulders captured the warm sunlight, as did his muscular torso, rotated slightly over solidly planted left leg, hip thrust up and forward.

"Provocative," I thought as I moved closer and continued to gaze at him: Neptune. His right hand, low and indifferent, grasped the famous trident. I approached, squinting from the sun. Finally close enough to feel his immensity and hear the fountain's splashing water, I said, "You remind me of Michelangelo's David, but you are not a beautiful, innocent youth. Beautiful? Yes, no, perhaps handsome and mature, definitely seductive."

Water streamed down from the urns held by the four cherubs who perched at the top of each corner of the great god's pedestal, filling expectant half-shells at the next level. It squirted noisily into the square pool below from the breasts of four kneeling river nymphs bent back upon their fleshy tail fins, at once suggestive and vulnerable.

Bologna Reflections

The Flemish sculptor Giambologna came to Bologna from Florence in 1563 to create the god. Tommaso Laureti, an architect from Palermo, designed the fountain's base. I wondered what Neptune was doing there, as the rev and growl of motorini, the whir of Fiats, and the screech of brakes mingled with echoes of spilling water. Why a god of the sea in land-locked Bologna? Perhaps the rivers and canals of her past had made her a city of water, guarded by Neptune over the centuries.

I walked around the god slowly. His muscular bulk, well-defined and taut, trapped centuries of unspent energy. I sat on the wide stone steps of the adjacent Palazzo Re Enzo, mulling over the myths of the gods, their wars, seductions, and their powers over us, my face and bare arms soaking up the afternoon's warmth. Neptune had caused terrifying tremors by raking the rocks and the earth with his trident, just as Bologna's university scholars had unleashed intellectual and moral tremors that shook the foundations of medieval thought. There could be many reasons, I suppose, behind the choice of Neptune.

Rousing myself from the bookish reveries of the lazy afternoon, I set off in delicious solitude on a slow walk under Bologna's lovely porticoes, losing myself among the gold and earthy ocher of her palazzi and the zigzag of their red tiled roofs. I would find the city's hidden canals and towers of the ancient past. I would search out quiet treasures. Like the provocative Neptune, Bologna's charm can be very seductive for those who stroll leisurely through her most ancient neighborhoods.

~

The city's gracious social life is blooming again. Stores gradually reopen and people are busy with their afternoon activities. Bologna once boasted a canal system connecting it with the Adriatic Sea. Used to transport people and goods and to power the city's mills and silk looms, especially during the Middle Ages and Renaissance, the waterway system flowed between the Fiume Reno in the west and the Savena in the east. I hope to discover the hidden Canale Navile and a host of twelfth century towers along the way. They reached their most splendid level between the twelfth and thirteenth centuries, when they numbered roughly one hundred in the Città Rossa. About twenty still remain.

Following Via dell'Indipendenza north, I turn right just before the cathedral of San Pietro at the corner of Via Altabella and enter another world of narrow lanes, timeworn and tired gray. Just as I soaked in the sunshine at Neptune's fountain I slow down to immerse myself in the colors of Bologna, the gray-white of gypsum, the golden tan of sandstone, and the rosy earth tones of the clay. Past the bell tower of the cathedral of San Pietro and the Palazzo Acivescovale (Archbishop's Palace), both symbols of the Roman Catholic Church's historical presence in the city, I notice on the right the Torre Altabella/Azzoguidi (Via Altabella 15) jutting up from the narrowness of Via Altabella. The slender, brown-gray sentinel is sandwiched in among windowless russet and gold palazzi. The Azzoguidi family built the Torre Altabella in the twelfth century for prestige and defense. Its name means high and beautiful and, unlike Bologna's other towers, it is truly perpendicular.

At Via Sant'Alò, I turn left and the Torre Incoronata soars high up just ahead (Via Albiroli 7). Built by the Prendiparte family in the twelfth century, its name comes from the crown-like design etched close to the top of the slim tower. Red geraniums spill out of window boxes under brown-shuttered rectangles of glass climbing up its flank. The street level entrance at the middle cuts through the thickness of giant selenite blocks that form its base. Above it are the typical bricks of the time, made from rich, brown clay and layered with the grime of history. In the eighteenth century, prisoners of the archbishop were incarcerated here.

I follow Via Albiroli to the right and then to the left as it twists and winds, discovering the Torrecasa Guidozagni. The squat *torrecasa* of the Guidozagni family also served as a house, as its name suggests. Built in the 1200s, its height was reduced in 1487.

Tranquility permeates the neighborhood but occasionally a heavy door slams, neighbors greet one other on the way to the afternoon market, or someone's hard-heeled shoes strike the stone passage to interrupt the stillness. When Via Albiroli meets Via Goito, I see Palazzo Bocchi on the left (Via Goito 16). Achille Bocchi built the palazzo in 1546. The Hebrew and Latin inscriptions that decorate its facade are striking. On the left a passage from Psalm 119 declares, in Hebrew: "Oh Lord protect me from the lips of the untruthful and from deceitful language." On the right a Latin verse from the First Letter of Horace says "You shall reign, they say, if you act righteously." Timeless messages hide in the back streets of the old city.

Via Albiroli meets Via Marsala where Casa Grassi (Via Marsala 12) has endured since the thirteenth century. The portico of tall wooden pillars makes it immediately recognizable as one of the oldest structures remaining in Bologna. Across the street low wooden posts support the portico at Via Marsala 17 and 19, as well. It's easy to imagine medieval Bologna in the dampness of these narrow streets bordered by little mismatched houses and low porticoes.

I turn left on Via Marsala from Via Albiroli and follow it until it meets Via Piella, and then turn right. Strains of Mozart filter out of an open window. Magenta impatiens cascade over the edge of a green window box and a white curtain swings lightly in the breeze. Gold and russet stucco remnants of antique houses spatter the oldest streets of Bologna.

Canals once cut through here where streets crisscross today. Although no evidence of waterways is apparent in any direction, I head to Via Piella 16 where a small window, shuttered closed, allows a glimpse of the old city's canal. En route, the Porta Govese or Torresotto dei Piella rises up ahead. The old gate, part of the second circle of city walls that protected Bologna from the late twelfth century on, looks just a little tilted, its legs stretching wide over Via Piella. At the top, another white-curtained window with another flower-filled window box signals present-day inhabitants.

Passing under the gate and ahead on Via Piella, I find the Window of Canale Navile on the left. A bridge under my feet crosses the mostly subterranean canal. A slice of blue sky and a band of rushing water flows down below when I open the small, wooden, graffiti-covered shutter. I imagine the bustling life on the waterways and the silk trade that made Bolognesi merchants wealthy and powerful during the Middle Ages. I imagine canal boats loaded with giant blocks of white stone from Dalmatia. The Bolognesi used them to build the foundation of the church dedicated to their beloved patron, San Petronio. I close the small shutter carefully to keep the surprise intact and cross to the other side of the bridge where cascading water inspires images of a life with people-crowded bridges, where the smack of water against stone fills my ears instead of the clamor of cars and motorini. The water is flowing in the canals because it is springtime and rain has been plentiful. Then I turn, leaving behind another of the quiet treasures hidden in modern Bologna.

North on Via Piella, I next turn right on Via Righi, which changes name to Via delle Moline at Via Alessandrini. At Via Capo di Lucca the Canale Navile leaves the city, but a gate prevents entrance into the access alley. However, the rushing water roars after a good rain and fills the air on Via delle Moline, as it has since ancient times.

Bologna Reflections

Then I notice the crowd both inside and outside the Gelateria Moline (Via delle Moline 13). Perhaps a little gelato research is called for. Crema and pistachio, or chocolate and strawberry? What should I try? I decide on the former, my usual test for a first visit, and I sit at a tiny table, savoring the rich confection, listening to the chatter of the other patrons, mostly university students, and the splashing water of the canal in back. I pick up my pack, shivering just a little from the chill of the gelato, as the sun begins to wane in the late afternoon. I arrange my scarf up close around my neck and move on before it gets too late to enjoy the rest of the neighborhood.

Next I turn left onto Via Oberdan from Via delle Moline and go toward the city center. Small stores sell everything from cheese to house improvements. Bar delle Acque (Via Oberdan 43) promises a view of the canal from inside, on top of it. Meanwhile, the church of San Martino tempts me. It was originally built in the thirteenth century while its present facade dates from 1561.

The interior resembles many of Bologna's other Gothic churches. I search out a few of the individual works of art hidden here. *Madonna del Carmine* by Jacobo della Quercia (1374–1438) stands on a pedestal on the left wall of the first chapel. Francesco Francia's *Madonna e santi* (1450–1518) and a *Deposizione* by Amico Aspertini (1475–1552) hang over its altar. On the right wall, fragments of *Natività*, a fresco by Paolo Uccello (1397–1475), are visible.

San Girolamo by Ludovico Carracci (1591), impressive in dimension and design, hangs over the fourth altar, further along on the left side. I imagine the breeze caused by the pallid angels' huge wings as they swoop over the massive figure of the saint in the dark space.

Lorenzo Costa's *Assunta* (1506) is suspended over the fifth altar, followed immediately by the *Madonna col Bambino* by Simone da Bologna

80

(fourteenth century) enshrined in a burnished gold frame. Fragments of a fresco by Vitale da Bologna (fourteenth century) cover the left front corner of the church. Vitale always managed to represent the human figure with soft sweetness and drama. Here I see Abraham gathering the blessed ones in his arms, the damned in hell, the apostles at the Last Supper, and various other figures and architectural elements. A fragment of Vitale's *Crocifisso*, just on the other side of the main altar, demonstrates the same human quality in the face of Christ. The figure projects calm and sleeplike tranquility, not pain and suffering.

I exit from the side of the church, just past the painting of Santa Teresa, onto Via Marsala, where I look up at the lunette over the outside door. The fifteenth century terracotta relief by Francesco Mazzini shows St. Martin of Tours covering the poor with his cloak.

Then I return to Via Oberdan and turn left, continuing toward the city center. Walking under the gentle curve of the long, pillared porticoes, I feel the interior space reaching out, inviting me to enter. A stop at a card or gift shop often evolves into a pleasant visit. Tempting pastries, piles of handmade tortellini, tortelloni, ravioli, bins of oily black olives, hooks of hanging Parma Prosciutto, and plump ovals of Mortadella Bolognese insist that I shop for dinner.

Heavily populated, the porticoed street bristles with life. The clatter of cups and saucers at each corner bar, the inevitable zoom of Vespas, and the animated voices of neighbors exchanging *due parole* outside the doorway of the tiny shops animates the neighborhood.

As I pass the little church of San Nicolò degli Albari, I look to the right and notice the fourteenth century Casa Azzoguidi and its portico, supported by thick wooden posts. The stained glass rosette window must have allowed streams of multicolored cobalt blue, purple, red, and golden light inside to play

Bologna Reflections

on the walls of the family's quarters. Finally, I head back to Via Rizzoli, leaving behind hidden towers, and the seductive images and sounds of Bologna's past, and present too.

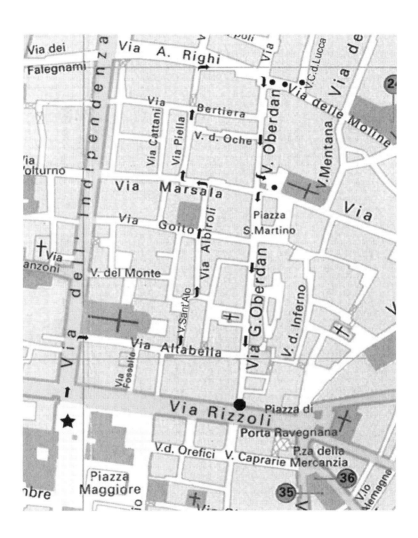

Map for *Seduction*

Figure 16. Voltone dei Malvasia, over Via del Carro

Neighborhood Collage

I f I stand in Piazza Giuseppe Verdi and turn around in place, looking high above the confusion and then closely at the world around me, a haphazard collage materializes, an assortment of colors, shapes, and textures. The piazza reflects the currents of city life that coexist in the neighborhood. University students crowd the space, motorini zoom by, and my path most assuredly crisscrosses yours.

The scene is chaotic and sometimes dingy. In front of the elegant Teatro Comunale the homeless ask for change while street musicians pick at guitars and stroke violin strings. Insistent vendors barter colorful beaded bracelets and exotic scarves for my cash. Fingers of the sweet, heavy smoke of patchouli incense perfume the air as I pass by. University students clad in up-to-the-minute grunge, with pierced everything and magenta or orange hair, pass easily by those outfitted in skirts, jackets, boots, and coifs lately arrived from Milano or Paris.

Up high I see ancient rectangular house towers peeking out over the modern scene and delightful patches of blue sky, yellow streams of light, and peach, mauve, and violet slices of masonry. There are curves and straight lines in Piazza Giuseppe Verdi, circles and boxes, clamoring shouts and lyrical refrains. The spirit of "live and let live" reigns.

Bologna Reflections

This neighborhood speaks of a past connected to power and wealth. It speaks of a long relationship with the university. It speaks of a present that is lively and controversial. Across from the Teatro Comunale the remains of the Bentivoglio stables accommodate a bar. The old barracks of the once powerful family's private soldiers are next door. The back of the basilica of San Giacomo Maggiore, adjacent to the rosy pink end of the delicate portico, shows a crenellated section of the Cerchia dei Mille, which once protected Bologna as a medieval city. The patchwork of past and present also extends outward from the piazza.

Giovanni II Bentivoglio became one of Bologna's most well known leaders and, in the fifteenth century, this neighborhood was his banking family's domain. Giovanni II's term of power (1463–1506) represented a relatively calm period in the normally tempestuous history of the city. Because of his wealth and prestige, important artists like Francesco Francia, Lorenzo Costa, Jacobo della Quercia, Nicolò dell'Arca, and even a young Michelangelo received commissions and worked in Bologna. He financed the elegant Renaissance portico that flanks the church of San Giacomo Maggiore on Via Zamboni, where the medallions of the delicately carved frieze hold his effigy. According to historical records, his immense palazzo of nearly 300 rooms, located where the Teatro Comunale is today, once dominated the quarter. It was destroyed by the masses in 1506. The Bentivoglio's powerful enemies, including the Malvezzi family, led by Pope Julius II, ran them out of Bologna. Today's Via del Guasto, which means "broken," refers to the total destruction of the palazzo and its contents. Palazzo Bentivoglio's tower is visible in Francesco Francia's *Madonna del terremoto* (1505), a fresco in the Sala d'Ercole of the Palazzo Comunale in Piazza Maggiore.

Via Zamboni, the quarter's main thoroughfare, connects Piazza Giuseppe Verdi to Piazza di Porta Ravegnana and the center of Bologna. It has formed the main axis of the University of Bologna district since the time of Napoleon. Before that, other influential families, besides the Bentivoglio, flaunted their power and wealth and controlled the fortunes of the city from their elegant palazzi. Now, during the day and at night, a rush of people and vehicles crowds it.

Many of the palazzi in the neighborhood house public offices, so during the week it is possible to explore the buildings. Just a few steps inside the portone will often allow the glimpse of a magnificent stairway, an unexpected garden, an impressive sculpture, or a fountain spurting streams of water. Palazzo Malvezzi Campeggi (Via Zamboni 22) at the corner of Via Marsala was probably designed by Andrea and Giacomo Formigine in the sixteenth century. Its porticoes complement those of the basilica of San Giacomo Maggiore across the street. Today it houses the university's law school.

Palazzo Magnani (Via Zamboni 20) offers a cycle of glorious frescoes, *The Foundation of Rome*, by the Carracci family artists. Palazzo Malvezzi de' Medici (Via Zamboni 13) across the street is a sixteenth century edifice rich with art and architectural detail. Palazzo and Casa Malvasia (Via Zamboni 16) includes the Voltone dei Malvasia. Its mask with the gaping mouth once spouted wine to the crowd below in celebration of the appointment of a family member to the post of Gonfaloniere di Giustizia, the city's highest official of justice. Palazzo Paleotti (Via Zamboni 25) boasts a beautiful courtyard from the time of Giovanni II Bentivoglio.

The graceful Cà Grande dei Malvezzi (Largo Trombetti 4) embellishes the space that opens up from Via Zamboni with the rhythm of its arched portico, windows, and delicately carved decorations. Restructured in the mid-fifteenth century by Virgilio Malvezzi, it is headquarters for the University of Bologna, along with Palazzo Poggi just around the corner. A short distance into the Largo Trombetti, opposite the Ca' Grande dei Malvezzi, is Via San

Bologna Reflections

Sigismondo, named after the little church in its tiny piazza. A diminutive, sun-bleached column with a tilted metal cross on top nudges up against the gingery orange end of an equally squat portico. The pillar stands askew, unmarked, and just a little weary from the passage of time.

Palazzo Poggi (Via Zamboni 33) was designed by Pellegrino Tibaldi and was constructed in 1550. In 1803 the seat of the University of Bologna was moved here from the Archiginnasio. Today it accommodates university offices as well as a variety of museums and artistic treasures. The statue of Hercules by Angelo Piò, the ceilings decorated with mythological subjects by Pelligrino Tibaldi, the Biblioteca Universitaria (a library of the University of Bologna), and the Academy of Science (entrance at Via Zamboni 31) are some of its offerings.

These magnificent palazzi and the basilica of San Giacomo Maggiore lay bare the riches and influence of the families who once lived here. The basilica, which stretches along the street toward Piazza Rossini, and the adjacent Oratorio di Santa Cecilia (Via Zamboni 15) each contain works by important artists who worked in Bologna, most of them during the Renaissance. San Giacomo Maggiore was built at the behest of the Augustinians from 1267 to 1315. The order still maintains a relationship with the complex. Giovanni II Bentivoglio financed the portico (1477–81) that runs along Via Zamboni. In addition to the neighborhood's powerful Bentivoglio family, others, including the influential Malvasia, Magnani, and Poggi families, also sponsored chapels, commissioning important artists to decorate them.

Lorenzo Costa's *Madonna dei Bentivoglio* (1488) originally adorned the Bentivoglio chapel in the apse of the basilica and provides an important portrait of them. Sometimes it has been moved to the adjacent chapel. Francesco Francia's *Madonna in Trono con Angeli e Santi* (1494) also graces the chapel. The Poggi chapel (1555), designed by Pelligrino Tibaldi, contains *Elemosina di San Alessio* by Prospero Fontana (1576).

88

Some of the other important pieces found in San Giacomo Maggiore are *Il Crocifisso* (1370) by Simone de' Crocifissi, *L'Incoronazione della Vergine* (1420) and *Il Crocifisso* (1426) by Jacobo di Paolo, a *Polittico* (1344) by Paolo Veneziano, *San Rocco* (1602) by Ludovico Carracci, and the exceptional marble sarcophagus of Galeazzo Bentivoglio (1438) by Jacobo della Quercia.

The fresco cycle celebrating the lives of Santa Cecilia and San Valeriano in the Oratorio di Santa Cecilia (Via Zamboni 15) was created by some of those same artists working in Renaissance Bologna. Lorenzo Costa (1460–1535), Amico Aspertini (1474–1552) and Francesco Francia (1450–1518) decorated its walls with ten scenes of the young saints' lives. The cycle was painted during 1505 and 1506 under the patronage of Giovanni II Bentivoglio. The three artists' styles complement each other, balancing the languid and sentimental with the strong and robust.

Bologna's Conservatorio di Musica G.B. Martini is located in the ex-convent of the Augustinian monks, next door to the church in Piazza Rossini. Through the cloister and up the elegant stairway I find concert spaces and the Museo Civico Bibliografico Musicale, the archive for a vast collection of rare and precious musical manuscripts. A mere walk by the building along Via Benedetto XIV often provides an opportunity to enjoy the music of the school's students, a surprise concert that floats out from the open windows above. In the late afternoon the bells of San Giacomo Maggiore sometimes join in with their song as well, one that carries out over the roofs and down the alleys of the quarter.

The Pinacoteca Nazionale (Via delle Belle Arti 56) is also close by, where Via Zamboni meets Via delle Belle Arti. The frenzied activity of Via Zamboni and Piazza Verdi does not normally intrude upon the calm of Via delle Belle Arti. It's possible to admire the occasional noteworthy palazzo and the Accademia di Belle Arti (Via delle Belle Arti 54) here, but the houses are

Bologna Reflections

generally more typical of a working class neighborhood in their smallness and simplicity. The porticoes are low and Bologna's usual shades of yellow and russet tinge the setting. A number of quiet bars offer refreshment and the opportunity to have a quiet conversation. Facets of a neighborhood. A collage that connects the pieces that are Bologna.

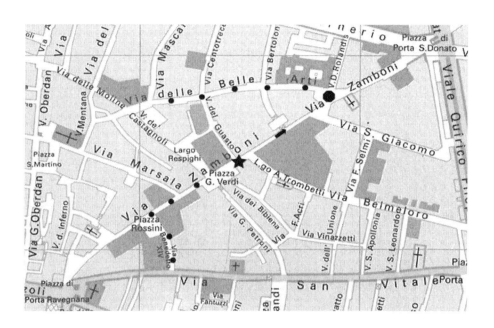

Map for *Neighborhood Collage*

Figure 17. Casa Volta-Figallo, Piazza della Mercanzia 1

At the Crossroads

Piazza di Porta Ravegnana, a focal point of Bolognese life since medieval times, lies at the very center of the city. An illustration from a manuscript held in Bologna's Museo Civico (*Il Mercato di Porta Ravegnana a Bologna*, from *Matricolae societatis draperorum, no. 93*), shows the piazza as it was in the fourteenth century. Trade thrived there at the intersection of three important streets—Via Zamboni (then called Via San Donato), Via San Vitale, and Via Mercato di Mezzo. It thrived in the adjacent Mercato di Mezzo (today's Via Rizzoli), which begins at the corner of Strada Maggiore. Important trade arteries opened up here: Via Caprarie and the little streets filled with merchants and artisans in the Quadrilatero, Via Castiglione, and Via Santo Stefano. Until the beginning of the eighteenth century, the Canale di Savena, with its waterway traffic, edged Via Castiglione.

The vivid illustration shows the bristling market life that filled the square. I imagine the sound of the Canale di Savena as it splashes just around the corner where Via Castiglione passed, while hawkers squawk, scrounging pigs grunt, chickens scrabble, and horses with their riders hustle out of Bologna on the Via Emilia. Shoppers, their heads covered in soft white caps and sheer, gauzy veils, barter with merchants clad in long blue and red robes. Fluid, draping fabrics hang off poles and rods in the stalls under the shadow of the towers. Cardinal red, royal blue, every nuance of white, and tints of brown color the world portrayed in miniature. Looking at the piazza now, thinking of the artist's representation, I see the stout bolts of cloth, men with hefty loads, long wooden plank worktables, rough leather satchels in a pile, drums, barrels, and bins. The breeze carries the murmur of friendly banter and spirited negotiations. A poor, scraggly fellow dressed in brown and shoeless, caught in the act of stealing, struggles to escape his fate against the backdrop of medieval Bologna, her familiar red tile roofs visible in the distance.

The layers of Bologna's history reach deep here. Piazza di Porta Ravegnana marked the eastern edge of the Roman city. Later it was just inside the first protective wall of selenite, built between the fifth and eighth centuries. Via Rizzoli was a narrow street called Via Mercato di Mezzo in the fourteenth century, and the gentle arch of the Ponte Romano (Roman Bridge) stretched over the Torrente Aposa, the natural waterway that traversed the city from the south. They can still be identified in tours of the subterranean hollows of the river and canals that run under modern Bologna.

Beyond the bridge lay Porta Ravennate, one of the city's most ancient gates, which opened up the first city wall of selenite. One of the crosses of Sant'Ambrogio, *La Croce degli Apostoli* (*the Cross of the Apostles*), was here as well.

Today's visitors to the piazza focus their attention on the city's famed two towers. The companion towers have been looking down upon the city and its inhabitants for nine centuries. Built for military purposes and as symbols of the prestige for the Asinelli and Garisenda families, the two towers once had many companions in the piazza. The Asinelli family constructed their tower from 1109–19. Later, in the fourteenth century, it served as a prison. Looking straight up its height I imagine a cage dangling from the edge with the Prior of Santa Maria degli Angeli inside: punishment for conspiring against the city. For centuries visitors have climbed the 498 steps to the top (320 feet) to see a magnificent panorama of Bologna and the surrounding countryside. Today a boutique specializing in articles made by Bolognese artisans and artists occupies the ground floor of the tower. In times past when the piazza, known then as Piazza Padella, resounded with the clamor of vendors selling copper pots and utensils, one might have come here to purchase fabrics, carpets, or copper pans.

The Torre Garisenda (154 feet) was built at about the same time as the Asinelli. Over time, as the earth settled, the structure began to lean menacingly. In 1360 government official Giovanni da Oleggio decreed that it must be shortened. Dante evoked the leaning tower in his *Inferno*, where he compared it to the tipping giant Antaeus frozen in a block of ice:

> The way the Carisenda seems to one
>   who looks up from the leaning side when clouds
>   are going over it from that direction,
>
> making the whole tower seem to topple—so
>   Antaeus seemed to me in the fraught moment
>   which I stood clinging, watching from below
>
> as he bent down; while I with heart and soul
>   wished we had gone some other way, . . .
>   (Canto XXXI vv. 136–43)

Perhaps thanks to Oleggio's handiwork, it no longer seems so dangerous to stand beneath the tower on the leaning side, where a plaque fixes Dante's words to the wall.

Modern tourists gawk at the towers, friends meet at their feet, and pedestrians, bicycles, cars, and buses arduously negotiate the intersecting streets below. A statue of the city's patron San Petronio stands on a pedestal below the towers after a long absence from the piazza. The statue by Gabriele Brunelli was commissioned in 1683 by the powerful Drapers' Guild, which held court in Piazza di Porta Ravegnana. In 1871 the work was moved to the basilica of San

Bologna Reflections

Petronio, where it remained until October 4, 2001, when the city chose the saint's feast day to return the statue to its traditional station. At that time, a small oratorio behind the Torre Garisenda reopened. Here one may view a fresco by one of Bologna's early artists, Lippo di Dalmasio (1352–1415), *La Beata Vergine delle Grazie* (*Blessed Virgin of the Graces*).

Producers and vendors of silk and other fabrics thrived in medieval and Renaissance Bologna. The Palazzo degli Strazzaroli (1466–96, Piazza di Porta Ravegnana 1), the headquarters of the Draper's Guild, sits opposite Torre Garisenda. A statue of San Girolamo, the patron of the trade, stands in the center of the facade where a continuously burning lamp once honored him. A bell affixed nearby called guild members to council meetings. The balcony was added in 1620, while the statue of the Madonna by Gabriele Fiorini, *La Madonna della nicchia*, was placed in the alcove under the overhang in the second half of the sixteenth century. Usually a red drapery covers the statue but it is exposed on special occasions and for a period every May when the Madonna of the Santuario di San Luca is carried down from the Colle della Guardia to bless the city.

Until recently, the Antica Farmacia Due Torri occupied the corner storefront on the street level of the Casa Volta-Figallo (Piazza della Mercanzia 1), ministering to the needs of Bolognesi as one *farmacia* or another had done since the early sixteenth century. According to the notary Battista Bovi, Vespiano Pocapenna bought a shop from Count Melchiorre Manzoli on June 14, 1518, in order to establish a *spezieria*, an early pharmacy and the forebear of the Antica Farmacia Due Torri. The records say that it was situated "under the arch of San Bartolomeo of Porta Ravegnana at the corner of Via Santo Stefano and of Strada Maggiore, facing the Torre Asinelli."

Walking into the establishment was like taking yet another step back in time. Its rich wooden counters reflected the light that entered from the beveled glass window of the elegant wooden door. Old beams traversed the painted wood ceiling whose partitioned sections narrated the story of the past: robed professors from the ancient university teaching their attentive students, chemists mixing their potions, physicians ministering to their patients, doctors approaching turreted cities on horseback. The pharmacy's wooden cabinets are empty now; the enterprise has moved to Via San Vitale 2. With melancholy and a certain passion, the pharmacist, Doctor Giovanni Falanelli, leans over the modern counter of his new pharmacy and discusses the ancient space now occupied by a Timberland store. The brightly lit space does still offer a glimpse of the past through the painted scenes depicted there.

The Palazzo della Mercanzia, built to be the seat of the Corporazioni dei Mercanti e dei Cambiatori (Guilds of the Merchants and Money Changers), adorns the piazza it stands in. Built from 1384–91 in the late Gothic style, the palazzo was designed by Lorenzo da Bagnomarino and Antonio di Vincenzo. The statues of San Petronio, San Francesco d'Assisi, San Domenico, and San Procolo, Bologna's protector saints, which once stood in the niches on the facade, have been replaced by copies as has the statue of Justice. The originals are now in the Museo Civico Medieval. The loggia, said to have been the first of its kind to be built in Italy, was used for unloading the goods that arrived at the city's customs office on boats that navigated the Canale di Savena. Before the palazzo was constructed, taxes were collected at the *gabella* (customs office) in the Case Seracchioti (Piazza della Mercanzia 2–3).

I imagine a guild official standing in the marble pulpit on the front of the building, reading the declarations and sentences of the Tribunale dei Mercanti (Court of the Merchants) and stirring up desperation in some and relief in others. The palazzo was built during the Signoria of Giovanni II Bentivoglio in the fifteenth century, and thus the heraldic shields of both Bologna and the Bentivoglio family decorate the lunette above the entrance.

Bologna Reflections

This relatively small space, this crossroads, is full of possibilities. I stand in place and spin around, allowing my eyes to take in everything: the towers, palazzi, saints, rushing crowds, and traffic. I am dizzy, of course—not only from the silly spin but also from the layers of history to consider buried in the stones underneath.

Map for *Crossroads*

Figure 18. Streetscape

Labyrinth

"Discovering the Jewish Ghetto in the dark and without a map was easy, " I thought, anxious to find my way back in the daylight. One night I attempted to cross directly from Via Zamboni to Via Oberdan and assumed that Via del Carro would connect the two. I ended up taking a roundabout route home that evening because the two streets do not link up directly in the neighborhood. In the process, I stumbled on a corner of the city that called up images of medieval Bologna and recommended a daytime visit.

By day, with a map and some basic information, the Jewish Ghetto does not seem like such a maze of dark streets, low porticoes, gloom, and musty air. Getting lost can often yield pleasant possibilities as it does here where a cobbled street that seems to cut straight across the neighborhood will probably make a sudden jog left or come to an inescapable dead-end stop. Perhaps the best approach is, in fact, to wander without a set itinerary. Weekdays and Saturdays are best because on Sundays the neighborhood's small stores and workshops are shuttered closed.

Setting out from Piazza di Porta Ravegnana at the foot of the two towers, I pick up Via Zamboni. Students of the University of Bologna fill the street, forcing me to jockey here and there to get through. Automobiles and motorini add to the traffic commotion. I weave back and forth from crowded sidewalk to crowded via, crossing in front of the little church of San Donato (Piazza San Donato 13) toward Via del Carro, which is signaled by the Voltone dei Malvasia, an archway with a yawning mask high above the street. Before going under, I stop to remember the history of this place, imagining the clanking of the nighttime gate that would have clamped down hard to keep the Jews on the other side. The Malvasia family's grand pink palazzo, with its drooping claret window shades (Via Zamboni 16), rises up next to the archway. The neighborhood, including the Porta di Piazza di Porta Ravegnana, the two towers, and the little streets between today's Via Oberdan and Via Zamboni, were once Bologna's predominantly Jewish quarter. Then the city declared it their prison-like ghetto where gates and restrictions ruled their lives. The streets most associated with that past are today's Via de' Giudei (of the Jews), Via dell'Inferno (of Hell), Via Canonica (of the pastor's house), Vicolo San Giobbe (Alley of St. Job), Via del Carro (of the wheeled transport wagon), and Via Mandria (herd of beasts). The Ghetto's ancient synagogue was at Via dell'Inferno 16. Two other early synagogues were at Via San Vitale 65 and in Piazza Santo Stefano. Today's synagogue is in Via de' Gombruti 9 and the Jewish cemetery in Via della Certosa.

From my position under the mask darkness reigns even during daylight hours. The sun struggles to warm my shoulders and lighten my spirits once I cross under the *voltone* onto Via del Carro. The Casa Rampionesi-Reggiani on the left (Via del Carro 4) suggests a voyage back in time. Constructed in the twelfth century its portico, supported by pillars of wood, is an example of what the city's earliest porticoes looked like. Under the portico, above the grated window, I can see fragments of the Torrecasa Marcheselli's foundation, its doorframe of selenite, and a partial edge of decorative bricks that represents the ancient past.

Under the graceful archway opposite Casa Rampionesi-Reggiani, a little tunnel leads to Via Valdonica. At the corner where the street seems to end but actually continues to the left, the deep yellow Palazzo Pannolini (Via Valdonica 1/5) houses the Museo Ebraico.

At the museum's black metal gate, I ring the bell and enter another world. Written, visual, and audio explanations give me a brief history of the Jews in Bologna and Emilia Romagna to carry with me when I return to the neighborhood. The earliest archival reference to the presence of Jews in Bologna was in 1353. During the last half of that century they were primarily rag dealers and moneylenders, the economic activities the city allowed them to practice. By the year 1387, according to records, thirty-five Jewish families lived permanently in Bologna.

Their lives, the freedom they enjoyed, or the restrictions they endured depended upon the whims of those who wielded power over the city. The Roman Catholic Church ruled Bologna for centuries and often made decisions based on prejudice and intolerance toward the Jews who, regardless of the obstacles, played an important role in the economic life of the merchant city. Many of them were major bankers who transacted business alongside Christian bankers in the area around the two towers and under the portico of the Palazzo dei Banchieri near Piazza Maggiore. They, of course, also participated in the economic life within the walls of the Palazzo della Mercanzia, at the crossroads of the prosperous trade that made Bologna so important. By the fifteenth century, the Città Rossa became a center for Hebrew study and for Hebrew printers in the latter fifteenth and early sixteenth centuries.

Eventually the church authorities who ruled the city, disapproving of the Jewish community's significant role in the city's life and the good relations it enjoyed with its Catholic citizens, placed restrictions on the Jews. They were intended to "protect" the Christians from being tainted by interaction with the

Bologna Reflections

Jewish population. As early as 1417 the Papal authorities forced them to wear an identifying mark. In 1477 the men were required to wear a piece of yellow cloth in the form of a circle on their chest and the women a yellow veil on their hat or yellow earrings.

The Papal Bull issued in 1555 by Pope Paul IV, *Cum nimus absurdum*, created the Jewish Ghetto that restricted every aspect of life. Three gates, located at the entrance to Via de' Giudei, at Via Zamboni (under the archway decorated with the mask at Via del Carro), and in Via Oberdan (in the arch that faces Vicolo Mandria across from Vicolo Tubertini) controlled entry and exit. Later the church compelled them to leave Bologna and move to a few remote towns.

~

Once outside the museum's gate, I follow Via Valdonica straight ahead. The street is cobbled, narrow, and dark. It's easy to imagine walking on medieval streets, which was a more pungent world. Crumbled stucco exposes tired old bricks underneath. Dark brown beams support low, heavy porticoes. Dirty lemon-yellow, dirty gold, dirty bronze, dirty pumpkin, dirty melon paint the scene. Closed green shutters block out whatever light could penetrate inside the small houses. It is smelly, too. The grates that open from the base of the houses onto the already dark, modest sidewalk reek of damp, hidden places. When I look up, an occasional rooftop garden or little tower comes into view, adding touches of red and purple and green to the drabness.

At Via dell'Inferno I turn left. Glancing up, I glimpse the tall Torre Asinelli ahead. A plaque at Via dell'Inferno 16 commemorates the neighborhood's ancient synagogue. Continuing along Via dell'Inferno I enjoy peeking into little studios of artists and artisans. A shop refurbishes antique

104

picture frames in one and artists restore paintings and frescoes in another. Eventually I reach another dead end. To the left I note a high walkway between two buildings but decide to turn to the right onto Vicolo San Giobbe toward the sign for Ristorante da Benso, which hangs over the narrow passageway. Grimy centuries-old bricks crowd me and I feel hemmed in and uneasy yet exhilarated by the chance to experience the atmosphere of the ancient time.

When I arrive at the end of what seems to be a blind alley, I realize that I can escape to the left onto Vicolo Tubertini, named for the palazzo of the Tubertini family. An old tower rises up on my right and I stop, turning back for a moment to face the twelfth century Torre Uguzzoni and its elevated walkway on Vicolo Mandria. This is the heart of the Ghetto, once regularly closed to the outside world each night.

Similar walkways are prevalent in the Ghetto. Often a Jew's safety was threatened because of prejudice and intolerance; the walkways allowed them to move without danger from one edifice to the other. The dark corners and shadows outside harbored risks, even when they were captive inside the gates. Now, the walkway's windows have flower boxes dripping red and white flowers.

Pigeons nest on the ledges of the highest glassless windows of the tower. Randomly spaced window openings of different shapes and sizes hold stories of the past that for now are indecipherable. Going back the way I came to Vicolo San Giobbe, I continue to Via de' Giudei and, in a window straight ahead across Via de' Giudei, prints of Bologna's leaning towers, facades of churches, cobbled piazzas, and narrow evocative streets hang next to etchings of Judaic symbols. La Tarlatana (Via de' Giudei 1/c) offers a glimpse into a working print shop. The name refers to the cotton cloth used throughout the creation process. Striking prints of every size, from small bookmarks and cards to large engravings line the walls and sit in piles everywhere around. Russet, navy, aqua, and blue color fields of creamy white paper with imaginative cats and drooping flowers, along with the images of the ancient city. It's always difficult to resist doing some shopping for special gifts.

Outside the shop again, I leave the labyrinth of the Jewish Ghetto and head toward the cacophony that explodes in the frenetic modern life of Piazza di Porta Ravegnana.

Map for *Labyrinth*

Figure 19. Bologna's Shield

Popes, Princes—and My Parrucchiere-Filosofo

S trada Maggiore may be the street of popes and princes, but to me it is home to my favorite haircut, the beauty shop Parrucchiere da Carlo (23), where I have gone since 1998. Walking into the shop is like taking a trip into the past. It reminds me of the office of old Dr. Hebb, the kindly, bespectacled family physician who took care of us when I was a child growing up in Bellows Falls, Vermont. I can see him looking up over the top of the wire-rimmed glasses that slid down his long nose. An office visit usually meant getting a shot, but nonetheless I was fond him. A trip to da Carlo's reminds me of sitting in that old, stuffed, brown leather chair in the waiting room and looking forward to the Doctor's affectionate greeting. As a child I felt his gentleness and somehow understood his wisdom. My Bolognese *parrucchiere* Franco, the son of Carlo, is a philosopher.

Da Carlo's is full of objects from the past. A hand-styled ceramic plaque advertises that the owner is a "Parrucchiere Naturalista." Antique spray bottles with round rubber pumps and squat, embossed glass receptacles sit in a display window along with monster-sized brass scissors. Just inside the door rests a large, walnut-brown tabletop radio with round knobs as big as silver dollars. Aged, brown, tweedy fabric stretches over its sound box. It still works, as do others sitting here and there next to antique clocks and other collectables.

Bologna Reflections

A candelabrum, dripping crystal baubles, descends from the center of the rather low ceiling and robust hanging plants add a touch of green in corners and on top of the partitions that separate the front of the shop from the back.

The glass counter reminds me of the one at old Whitcomb's department store in Bellows Falls, except that instead of fancy, soft, white gloves or lacey handkerchiefs it is full of memorabilia connected with American baseball. The Signor Parrucchiere Franco, now in his seventies, has always been a devout fan of *il basbol*. He has played since his youth and is also an umpire. Bologna's national and international baseball expert, he can recall the game's statistics from both sides of the Atlantic Ocean.

When I enter the shop for a cut, my parrucchiere-filosofo Franco welcomes me, very formally, into the salon. Then the Signora Parrucchiera Franca ushers me, businesslike, into a small, well-lighted cubicle in the back all the while asking me questions about my most recent sojourn in Bologna. After she's seated me with much ceremony, he enters and proceeds to cut my short hair with little scissors—snip, snip, snip—as she busies herself out of sight. She then re-emerges to wash and style the coif, telling him gracefully where he needs to re-snip. Then she disappears again. He refines the cut with an authoritative snip or two and then she reappears to brush and blow and clean things up. Sometimes he comes back to smooth it out. Other times all is approved, and we are done. Teamwork, just like a baseball game.

The parrucchiere-filosofo cuts my hair the way I like it, and besides, I enjoy listening to him talk about Bologna—and life. Early on I asked him about doing a color rinse to perk up my gray-streaked hair. Then I discovered what the sign "Parrucchiere Naturalista" means. "You will have to find someone else to do your hair," he said. "I don't do color, and furthermore, rosso, red, is the most unnatural color for a woman to apply unless she is born with it."

I sat there quietly, so he went on. "You know," he said, "it's true, you have a little gray coming in your hair, but it does not make you look old. On the contrary, you are just as you should be. You are full of life and your skin and hair works together to accomplish it. We age. We age regardless. We cannot stop time. If we accompany time gracefully as it passes, we will look our best. A woman of seventy who colors her hair black still looks seventy, maybe even older. And a woman of thirty with graying hair still looks thirty. No, I wouldn't do it, if I were you, and I won't." That was the last time we discussed coloring my hair. I know that I could never return if I did so I haven't. I probably won't either, because I appreciate his point.

Since that first sermon I have listened to many other predications. His topics range from current life on Strada Maggiore and in Bologna to the general state of the world. I like it best when he talks about the places that used to be and the ones that still are, if one knows where to look. Meanwhile, he snips away and cleans the neckline with the old-fashioned, hand-powered hair clippers that perform perfectly, just like my mother's did when she trimmed my brother's neck at the end of a homemade haircut. To finish, the Signora hand-sprays my short-cropped hair using one of those fabulous bulbous decanters that most people just collect to show off in a curio cabinet.

I have other haunts on Strada Maggiore. I head to a truly majestic temple farther along the street: Santa Maria dei Servi (46). Built from 1346 to 1504, the basilica is lovely to approach from any direction, with its wide, graceful portico. Light fills its underside, while narrow, slim columns hold up its generous width with delicacy and ease. The portico creates an elegant square at the front of the church on Via Guerazzi and extends along Strada Maggiore to the end of the block.

The feast day of Santa Lucia is the thirteenth of December. Inside the basilica of Santa Maria dei Servi her statue floats in a lake of candles and flowers, while outside, under the portico, a festive holiday fair begins. During the first week of December, booths spilling over with goods suddenly appear, just in time for the Christmas shopping season. Bells, garlands, and wreaths hang everywhere and sit in bins and baskets on tiered counters, alongside colorful Nativity sets with stables and brightly painted figures of all sizes and qualities. Woolen scarves and gloves in rainbow colors hang near ribbed knitted sweaters and button-down vests. The sizzling aroma of Bolognese fast food fills the air: the *piadine* (flat tortilla-like bread from Romagna) overflowing with pork and cheese, grilled vegetables, and sausages. The sweet, sugary smell of freshly made, fluffy pink cotton candy, the piles of nougat torrone, the mounds of chewy taffy, and roasted and candied nuts call loudly as I maneuver under the crowded portico.

Inside the huge rusty red and cream Gothic basilica, the air hangs heavy with the scent of sweet incense. Its three naves soar toward heaven and a hush fills the holy place. A number of interesting works of art are hidden here. When I find a new one, the excitement reminds me of being on a treasure hunt and discovering something of value buried in an unexpected corner. *Lo sposalizio mistico di Santa Caterina* (*The Mystical Marriage of St. Catherine*) is by Lippo di Dalmasio (1352–1410) and I wonder if recent brides have placed the small, multicolored bouquets of flowers that lie in front of it. The same artist's triptych, a fresco framed in terracotta (1352–1410) looks across the aisle at patches of frescoes by Vitale da Bologna. When I deposit a coin in the box to illuminate the chapel holding Cimabue's *Vergine col Bambino e angeli* (*Virgin with Christ Child and Angels*, 1272–1301), a gift of Taddeo Pepoli to the friars, a golden light shines out gloriously from the painting. The fresco of Giovanni Lianori (fifteenth century) in the same chapel, *La Madonna e il Bambino tra i Santi Cosma e Damiano* (*The Madonna and Child between Saints Cosma and Damiano*) adds reds and blues to the unlit inner region. Then the soft roses and blues of

L'Annunciazione (*The Annunciation*) by Innocenzo da Imola (1497–1550) contrasts with the brooding, dark *Madonna della Salve Regina* donated by S. Filippo Benizzi (1285) that is placed under it. They hide in out-of-the-way corners. Who knows what I will find the next time I visit.

Royal pageants, both ecclesiastical and civic, used to unfold here along Strada Maggiore, whose imposing patrician palazzi once belonged to popes and aristocrats. The magnificent structures have high porticoes held aloft by massive columns and pillars. The decorative painting under the rooflines, details on the capitals of the columns, ornate balconies overlooking the street, carved friezes, terracotta window frames, and giant portoni create a majestic aura of wealth.

The details are overwhelming. I feel their overall grandeur as I walk under the elegant porticoes, first on one side and then the other. Little by little, I note small elements as I happen by. My perspective changes daily. Sometimes the sunlight draws attention to a window or a finely carved frieze I have never noticed before. Perhaps an enormous door suddenly opens to reveal a lovely garden or a dragon's head door fixture of burnished bronze catches my wandering attention. Sometimes I sit under the portico at a café and from that vantage point note the arches of the portico on the other side of the street. After dark I get a glimpse of their elaborately painted ceilings through first or second story windows left open to the night. I wonder if the inhabitants realize how often this vision has enriched my evening walk.

Palazzo Sorgi's (15–17) original thirteenth century portone might be the widest in Bologna. It is easy to imagine a horse-pulled wagon or two passing through from the street to the secluded inner sanctum. Casa Isolani (19) is one of the few remaining examples of a thirteenth century edifice. Its portico is held up by thirty-foot high oak trunks, which support the third floor. I join the groups of tourists and stand underneath the high portico looking for the three arrows that have been stuck there for centuries, according to legend and zealous tour guides. Today, stylish shops and restaurants fill the space inside, which also provides a convenient pass through to Piazza Santo Stefano.

In 2004 the Palazzo Andrini-Sanguinetti (34) became the home of the Museo Internazionale della Musica. The carefully restored edifice, with its splendid seventeenth and eighteenth century frescoes, is one of the best examples of Napoleonic and neoclassical architecture in Bologna. A large collection of books, paintings, and musical instruments are conserved and exposed in the impressive palazzo.

Palazzo Hercolani (45) was built in the eighteenth century. Its huge atrium leads back to an open courtyard and then to the lovely Giardino Alexander Dubcek on the left. A mushroom fountain spurts water quietly, while around it lovers gaze into each other's eyes, friends talk quietly, and students read in the tranquil green inner sanctuary. During the week it's possible to enjoy the quiet garden, look at the palazzo's grand staircase, or explore the courtyard because the palazzo is the seat of the University of Bologna's Department of Political Science.

Bartolomeo Provaglia designed Palazzo Davia-Bargellini (44) in the 1600s for Carmillo Bargellini. Two giant *telamoni* (figures) sustain the balcony on either side of the entrance. The one on left is by Gabriele Brunelli and the one on the right by his student Francesco Agnesini.

The palazzo is open for the public to enjoy because it houses the Museo d'Arte Industriale. The museum has accumulated a wide range of useful and decorative household and mechanical objects, musical instruments, and other items that would have been found in Bolognesi households, largely from the sixteenth to the eighteenth centuries. Going through it feels like rummaging around in my Grandma's attic.

I will never forget the first time I saw the paintings in the Galleria Davia-Bargellino, which is part of the museum's offerings. When I discovered Vitale da Bologna's fourteenth century *Madonna dei denti* (*Madonna of the Teeth*) in the gallery, I suddenly realized that even though his medium was paint on wood, his works in no way resemble those of the typical, stiff, celestial Madonnas and saints of the time. His are full of drama and movement. When did the Renaissance really begin in Bologna?

The handsome staircase designed by Giovan Giacomo Dotti (1730) climbs gracefully to the *piano nobile*, while the painted courtyard recalls *trompe l'oeil* of the eighteenth and nineteenth centuries when idealistic bucolic scenes and gardens evoked a world of luxury, wealth, and dreams.

An inscription at the corner of Strada Maggiore and Via Malgrado commemorates the incredible feat of architect Aristotle Fioravanti on August 12, 1455. He successfully moved the fifty-nine-foot Torre della Magione from Strada Maggiore 80 to the corner position. I can imagine myself in the crowd watching his son ride bravely at the top of the tower as it inched along the street and shouting my approval when the deed ended successfully for everyone: Fioraventi's pride still intact and his son as well.

I have saved my best secret about Strada Maggiore for last. After doing serious research, I discovered my favorite pistachio gelato at Gelateria dei Comercianti (23), next to da Carlo where Franco my parrucchiere-filosofo reigns. If it happens to be a very hot day in the late afternoon, they may even come by and offer us a complementary portion. Pistachio, per favore!

Bologna Reflections

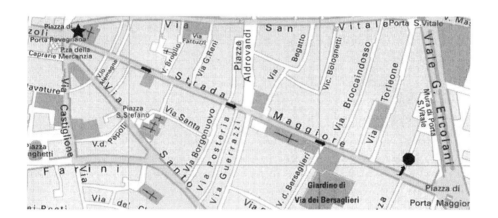

Map for *Popes, Princes—and My Parrucchiere-Filosofo*

Figure 20. Santo Stefano, Pilate's Courtyard

Pilgrimage

S naky ribbons of porticoes that line Via Santo Stefano usher the pilgrim to the Sanctuary of Santo Stefano, which presides graciously over its peaceful piazza. Pedestrians and bicyclists crisscross the triangular space formed by the gentle widening of the narrow street. A contemplative hush, a respite from the noise and rush of the clamoring city, welcomes us.

When the sun is setting and darkness descends over Bologna, I like to stand in the largely empty piazza and look up into the open windows of the elegant Renaissance palazzi of once illustrious Bolognese families. Here, too, if I am lucky and not all the drapes have been closed for the night, I see swatches of the colorful, frescoed ceilings of the illuminated rooms on the *piano nobile* that emerge through soaring windows. I imagine the day-to-day lives of the rich silk merchants and powerful town officials who inhabited the elegant palazzi, the conversations, music, laughter, and tears that filled these rooms.

I am always a pilgrim at Sancta Jerusalem Bononiensis, as the Sanctuary of Santo Stefano is sometimes identified, a reverent traveler to this holy place where tranquility reigns. Over the centuries pilgrims have arrived to honor its saints—Stefano, Vitale and Agricola, and Petronio—and for the special blessings associated with making the journey. I ask myself why I, too, often wander here, drawn to the spot that has been a sacred site for millennia. I come to feel close to Bologna's spiritual center. Even now the Bolognesi consider it the holiest place in their city. I come here to contemplate the past and to feel connected to it. I come to refresh my spirit, to enjoy the silence that allows me to touch my own soul. I have to admit though, I do sometimes come here just to buy my favorite peach preserves or honey made by the monks and sold in the little store.

The lack of documentation makes tracing the factual history of the Santuario di Santo Stefano difficult and explains the wealth of legends that circulate. Its name probably derives from the discovery in 415 AD in Jerusalem of the relics of Santo Stefano, the first Christian martyr. Sant'Ambrogio, archbishop of Milano, under whose jurisdiction the diocese of Bologna fell, consecrated a small chapel in his name here, close by a Roman temple to the Egyptian goddess Isis. He is believed to have constructed here a replica of Christ's sepulcher in Jerusalem. The nucleus of the Santuario di Santo Stefano began then.

Before that, however, in 393 AD, Sant'Ambrogio had already recovered the remains of Bologna's own first martyrs, Vitale and Agricola (304 AD), buried in an existing Jewish cemetery outside the first wall of selenite near the same Roman ruins. Some evidence suggests that even before the Christian edifices existed, pilgrims came from other parts of Italy and from across the Alps to venerate the relics of those early martyrs.

San Petronio, who became bishop in Bologna in 423 AD, took advantage of the religious fervor generated by the discovery of Vitale and Agricola's remains in Bologna and those of Santo Stefano in Jerusalem. He created a place to honor Bologna's saints in the little church already dedicated to Santo Stefano. Even from his time it is possible that monks and a monastery were associated with the place.

The fortunes of the sacred site went up and down according to the political climate of the city. When the Lombards won control over Bologna in 727 AD their King Liutprando named it the spiritual center of the diocese of Bologna. Eventually in the tenth century the Benedictine monks were given the shrine and it was enlarged and rebuilt numerous times.

The complex eventually consisted of seven churches, each with a different name, built from between 431 AD to the end of the sixteenth century. Known also as Sancta Jerusalem Bononiensis, the name refers to it as a representation in Bologna of the holy places connected to Christ's passion and death in Jerusalem.

Four churches remain after extensive restructuring over the centuries: the Chiesa del Crocifisso (Church of the Crucifix), the Chiesa del San Sepolcro (Church of the Holy Sepulcher), the Chiesa dei SS. Vitale and Agricola (Church of SS. Vitale and Agricola), and the Chiesa della Trinità or del Martyrium (Church of the Trinity or of the Martyrs). The museum and bookstore now occupy what was once called the Chiesa della Benda, referring to the veil of Christ's mother, another relic that San Petronio is said to have brought back from Jerusalem.

The first church one enters upon crossing the threshold from the piazza is the Chiesa del Crocifisso. The words "Sancta Sanctorum" (Holiest of the Holy), carved in the arched, brick strip over the main entrance to the complex, have welcomed visitors to this place for over 1,000 years. Darkness and the spicy sweetness of incense overwhelm the senses. Little cities of lights, candles lit in prayer, twinkle to the left and right. Flickering candles border *La Pietà* on the left aisle by Angelo Piò (1690–1769). In the dim light it is just possible to make out the crucifix by Simone de' Crocifissi which hangs down into the space over the stairway to the presbytery (about 1380). Simone left many such crucifixes around Bologna.

Bologna Reflections

I always stop in front of a fresco called the *Little Madonna of Paradise* by Michele Matteo (fifteenth century), which is on the wall in a dark corner lit by rows of tall, white candles in wrought iron holders. The image also lights the darkness with the Madonna's lovely, sweet, almond-shaped eyes and her soft smile. She wears a red tunic. Her very young face is framed by a midnight blue veil, the dark fabric woven through with fine gold. The child looks out, held in his mother's protective grasp, but it is the young mother whose eyes connect with mine. My coins clink-clank into the metal box as I prepare to light a votive candle, and I think of the sweetness of my own mother.

Legend plays with history in the sunken, dark eeriness of the crypt below it. Roman ruins were used in the building of this Romanesque vault (1019 AD), which houses SS. Vitale and Agricola's relics. A surprising harmony exists despite its having been being built using scavenged materials. The columns are of different styles and dimensions and were made to fit into place by laying slabs of stone underneath when necessary. Some of the capitals are simple while others are ornate. Legend has it that San Petronio brought the second column on the right—it is in two pieces and has no capital—home with him from Jerusalem in order to demonstrate Christ's exact height to the people.

From the Chiesa del Crocifisso I pass into the oldest of the complex's still extant churches, Chiesa del San Sepolcro, through a brown wooden door. The octagonal edifice terminates in a high, bricked cupola. A structure, mysterious and wonderful, dominates the cool space. My initial reaction is "What is this, and should I be here?"

This replica of Christ's sepulcher in Jerusalem sits inside a ring of twelve brick columns in clear reference to the twelve apostles and the twelve tribes of Israel. Seven of them are paired with black, cipolin marble ones, thought to be remnants of the ancient Roman Temple of Isis. In Roman times during the first century AD, the circular temple dedicated to the Egyptian

122

goddess Isis stood exactly where San Sepolcro is today. Erected over a natural spring by Calpurnia, a rich Bolognese woman, its water was, according to legend, sanctified by intermingling it with water carried from the Nile River. The Latin inscription in a strip of white marble embedded in the outside wall of the church of the Crucifix next door was found in the piazza in 1299 and confirms Calpurnia's commitment to the spiritual life.

In his zeal to create the sanctuary, San Petronio constructed a circular baptistery over the spring and used the vestiges of the Temple of Isis and relics he brought back from the Holy Land to construct this replica of Christ's sepulcher. The black column that stands alone outside the circle is said to be that of Christ's flagellation, another relic brought back by San Petronio from Jerusalem. Until quite recently this saint protector's remains were in the base of the sepulcher, but they have since been moved to the basilica of San Petronio.

From San Sepolcro I enter the fifth century Chiesa dei Santi Vitale ed Agricola. Shafts of diffused light filter through brown-streaked, creamy, alabaster slits in the narrow, rosy-gray apse. A heavy slab of white stone is supported by two plain circular structures in the sanctuary. The ends of two massive sarcophagi sit side by side and prop up the rear of the altar, simple and crude, like a sacrificial table in a pagan temple. The hollow darkness and the stony emptiness speak of antiquity, as do the smell and feel of cold and damp. Footsteps pound the hard pavement and the echoes fill the hollowness. All is white-gray stone and rosy-square bricks, arches and vaults, heavy, squat columns, barrenness, the stripped-down essence of early Christendom. Shadows defeat light and summon images of a past that reaches far beyond the appearances of today. These are the images of Bologna's ancient past that I carry with me when I leave her holiest site.

I cross San Sepolcro and exit outside into the Cortile di Pilato (Pilate's Courtyard), which takes its name from the giant, chalice-shaped marble basin that dominates the center. Its original place was in the Chiesa del Crocifisso. The basin is purported to be a gift of King Liutprando (730–740 AD) to the city of Bologna and once collected offerings from the faithful. Its name refers to Pontius Pilate's symbolic washing of his hands. On the outside wall of San Sepolcro, patterns imbedded in the bricks are visible. The checks, triangles, strips, circles, and stars of blue, purple, violet, mauve, rose, russet, brown, and cream stones create cosmic designs typical of the Middle Ages, symbolic motifs, steeped in magic and mysticism. I ponder those times as I approach the irresistible wall and wonder at the mysteries of the stars and circles and triangles, their connection to divinity and perfection in a far from perfect human world.

The place is awash in symbols. A crown, high up in the center of the wall, symbolizes Santo Stefano, the first martyr. Under the portico of the courtyard, a rooster dating back to the fourteenth century reminds the pilgrim of St. Peter's negation of Christ while a pair of scissors set into the wall remembers a tailor who asked that the emblem of his trade be placed near his burial site.

Past this courtyard lies another, the cloister of the Benedictine monastery attached to the complex. A seventeenth century well dominates the center of the space, which is surrounded by a graceful double loggia. The lower tier of the loggia was constructed between the tenth and eleventh centuries while the more ornate upper one dates to the thirteenth century. The fantastic capitals of the columns impressed Dante during his studies at the ancient university in 1285.

According to legend, Dante, inspired by two of the capitals, placed them in his *The Divine Comedy*. One appears in Canto X of the *Purgatorio* as a symbol of the weight borne by those who committed the sin of pride.

> True, those who crawled along that painful track
> were more or less distorted, each one bent
> according to the burden on his back;
>
> yet even the most patient, wracked and sore,
> seemed to be groaning: "I can bear no more!"
> (Canto X, vv. 133–37)

The other appears in Canto XX of the *Inferno* and represents the imposters who profess the art of divining and must walk with their necks stretched backwards over their shoulders.

> And when I looked down from their faces, I saw
> that each of them was hideously distorted
> between the top of the chest and the lines of the jaw;
>
> for the face was reversed on the neck, and they came on
> backwards, staring backwards at their loins,
> for to look before them was forbidden. . . .
> (Canto XX, vv. 10–15)

Dante was moved by this holy place. I wonder if he also wandered here, pulled by the inexplicable aura that has drawn pilgrims for millennia.

I always end up in the Chiesa della Benda where the museum and little store, operated by the Benedictine monks, allow me to peruse the ancient past by way of relics and art—and buy postcards, herbal tinctures, fruit preserves, and herbal teas. However, over the years I have recognized that the monks' succulent, unforgettable *marmellata di pesca* (peach preserves) is, by itself, always worth my journey.

Figure 21. Sarcophagus of Giovanni da Legnano, Detail

Fragments

T he courtyard of the fifteenth century Palazzo Ghisilardi-Fava (Via Manzoni 4) is defined by a lyrical Renaissance gallery whose arches are supported by four huge, stone corbels decorated with blooming flowers in relief. The thirteenth century Torre dei Conoscenti reaches up toward the sky opposite the gallery. Massive rectangular blocks of selenite from the first city wall, probably erected in the late fourth century, shape the south side of the tower. Before the seventh century two great arches of selenite no doubt created a lookout on the north side. When the sun is shining, the rocks flicker alive as flecks of mica catch the light. The *rocca* (fortress), the center of Imperial power in twelfth century Bologna, was located here before rebellious Bolognesi destroyed it in 1116. At certain locations inside the palazzo, which has housed the city's Museo Civico Medievale since 1985, one can see Roman ruins that lie underneath all the other layers of history in the neighborhood. Just as its collection exhibits many fragments of the city's antique past, this is an edifice where the ages mingle.

A decoration dating back to the thirteenth century surrounds a window in the internal wall at the base of the Torre dei Conoscenti. The red vine trails inside and around medieval bricks that open up over the lower level of the museum. Random strokes of deep blue punctuate the design, suggesting the beauty of other details that have been worn away with time. Fragments of tombs of the ancient university's revered professors, especially from the fourteenth and fifteenth centuries, fill many rooms. The slabs of carved, creamy marble or gray-white stone of Istria show robed and capped students gazing in thought, discussing points of law, writing notes, or listening to the lecturing professor. Bonifacio Galuzzi is represented, along with Giovanni da Legnano and others who made the early university famous.

This is the "temple of my muse," for it inspires my discovery—and story of Bologna. The Palazzo Ghisilardi-Fava itself is part of the tale. The Conoscenti, a powerful Bolognese family of the fourteenth century, built their tower and house on top of the already rich layers of Bologna's past. Because they eventually owned the entire block from Via Porta di Castello to Via dell'Indipendenza, more than one house existed. Their tower, discovered during twentieth century restorations, probably predated the elegant house that Alberto Conoscenti, treasurer of the independent Comune, constructed in the early 1300s. In later centuries the Ghisilardi and Fava families each built and rebuilt on the original plan and, in time, hid the Conescenti tower and earlier historical elements from view. In recounting the palazzo's history, I like to include my American friend Roy Fava, whose ancestors inhabited the elegant mansion. At least we like to think so!

At one time the entire area from the cathedral of San Pietro (Via dell'Indipendenza) and Via Altabella to Via del Monte shaped the vanished Piazza San Pietro. The cathedral represents the Roman Catholic Church in Bologna today but was once the symbol of its political power over the city as well. The Imperial fortress or castle, representing the power of the Holy Roman Empire, probably stood proudly on the little incline that forms the jagged passage between Via Parigi and the vaulted *porta* opening onto Via Montegrappa before it was destroyed in 1116. The neighborhood has always reflected the long-ago power of both the Empire and the Church in Bologna.

Other fragments of Bologna's past rest here and there in the streets that crisscross where the Imperial castle once stood. From the sidewalk on Via Manzoni, a look through the windows of Hotel Baglioni's restaurant (Via dell'Indipendenza 8) reveals the frieze painted by Annibale and Agostino Carracci, *Mito d'Europa* (1582–83). A swirl of color dances over the heads of stylish diners. Excavations under the hotel have revealed remains of the huge Roman commercial market or *macellum* of Bononia.

Across the street from Palazzo Ghisilardi-Fava, the lovely facade of Madonna di Galliera (Via Manzoni 3) stands out. Its origins date to the early fourteenth century. The facade, rich with worn away, tall sculptures of saints in high alcoves, was designed by Donato di Cernobbio and was completed between 1479 and 1510. The fifteenth century Casa Castelli-Benelli (Via Parigi 2) was once called Palazzo della Posta because in 1768 the building was used as the city's first post office as the old mail slot to the right of the portone still announces: *posta*.

Via Manzoni, with a little jig becomes Via Parigi and tiny Via Porta di Castello with a little jag, evolves into elegant Via Galliera. It was probably part of the *cardo massimo*, the primary north-south axis, of Roman Bononia. The countless shades of brown, russet, and gold are familiar today, as are the architectural details and the march of the giant porticoes into the distance. Via Galliera's impressive palazzi suggest a rich history. Important people lived here while key historical events unfolded. Once upon a time it formed the main north-south thoroughfare, while today historians still argue about the origin of its name. A variety of theories circulate. One proposes that after the Romans defeated the Gauls and forced them out of the city, their camp could have been located to the northwest of the city so the road leading to it would bear their name. Another suggests that Via Galliera was named after Galeria Faustina , a noble Roman woman.

Bologna Reflections

A walk on Via Galliera can turn into a treasure hunt. Strolling under the porticoes that line both sides of the street, I often cross back and forth, from one side to the other. From a distance a grand Renaissance palazzo looks magnificently elegant and up close promises exquisite details on columns, doors, and window frames—and maybe a peek into a quiet, green courtyard. Little things catch my attention: mullioned, arched windows, decorative friezes, terracotta borders, intricate ironwork, and imaginative capitals on a myriad of columns and pilasters.

The architecture and details in Via Galliera juxtapose irregular bits and shapes of centuries. Corinthian capitals on the columns of mid-sixteenth century Palazzo Torfanini's portico (Via Galliera 4) have fantastic heads that look out from each corner. Palazzo Tuate (6) was constructed at the beginning of the sixteenth century and is perhaps remembered best for its capital on the column at the corner of Via San Giorgio where I can search for the carved head of Giovanni II Bentivoglio. Perhaps it is a fragment of his palazzo, which stood in today's Piazza Verdi until angry citizens destroyed it in 1507. Meanwhile, the imposing, elaborately detailed Palazzo Aldrovandi-Montanari (8), with decorative ironwork at the windows, was once the seat of the famous Aldrovandi laboratory of ceramics. Palazzo Felicini-Fibbia (14), preserved almost entirely in its original form, is a good example of fifteenth century architecture of the Bentivoglio period. When it was restored in 1906, the terracotta of the facade was not touched. On the capitals the small family heraldic shields, with the fern of the Felicini family and the swan of the Ringhieri, were re-carved. In 1515 Leonardo da Vinci was a guest in the house along with Filiberta di Savoia. Bolognese legend says that while there he painted *La Gioconda* using the same Filiberta as his model, not Lisa di Francesco Giocondo. The unusual capitals of the columns supporting Palazzo Bonassoni's porticoes have figures that resemble babies with serpents' legs stretching out

130

from each side. In Casa Fava (34), Luigi Zamboni and Giovanbattista de Rolandis planned the unsuccessful revolt against the Papal States in 1795. The arched lintel of the portico of Casa de' Buoi (35), built in the 1400s, is richly decorated. The fourteenth century portico of Casa Belvisi (42) was rediscovered and restored in 1902, with significant pieces of the original architectural structure now visible.

The small church of the Madonna della Pioggia (of the Rain) sits in the corner of Piazzetta della Pioggia. People bustle back and forth between Via Marconi and Via Galliera by way of Via Riva di Reno, which once bounded the grand Canale del Reno in the prosperous merchant city. The church poked high up, surrounded by water. Called the church of San Bartolomeo until the fourteenth century, it was a hospital and orphanage. Then in 1516 the Bolognesi attributed the end of a drought to a fourteenth century sacred image of the Blessed Virgin found nearby and the church became known as Madonna della Pioggia. The miraculous image of the Madonna is invoked and carried reverently through the streets of the city during times of drought. Today, framed in gold, behind a thick glass screen, it stares out from its position over the main altar.

The church has been reconstructed many times but still retains its charm. Inside the dark interior, the devotion of people stopping by to pray in the silence always strikes me. A shepherd's strong hand caresses a resting lamb, while the Holy Family sits in the background of Agostino Carracci's *Presepio* in the first chapel to left of the entrance. In the far left front corner, a small room with a niche painted cobalt blue and flecked with little yellow stars, holds an ancient statue of the Madonna della Provvidenza, which was removed from the city wall in 1435. The space seems like a cave hidden in the safety of a holy place that time has forgotten, just as the church itself is a haven of peace while the modern world races by outside.

Bologna Reflections

When I imagine myself a fragment of Bologna's past in this neighborhood, I am invariably one of the fourteenth century students of the Alma Mater Studiorum remembered in the Palazzo Ghisilardi-Fava's Museo Civico Medievale. I choose a seat in the marble *Arca di Giovanni da Legnano*, signed by the Venetian brothers Jacobello and Pier Paolo Dalle Masegne. I become that dreamy student in one of the three remaining fragments, perhaps his daughter Novella, who is wrapped in a flowing gown and swirling scarf. I sit at a desk, head resting on left hand as the right one lays on a closed book. I am looking toward the honorable professor, but my eyes are gazing past him, perhaps because of the enchanting thoughts whirling around in my own imagination. After all, I am in the temple of my muse.

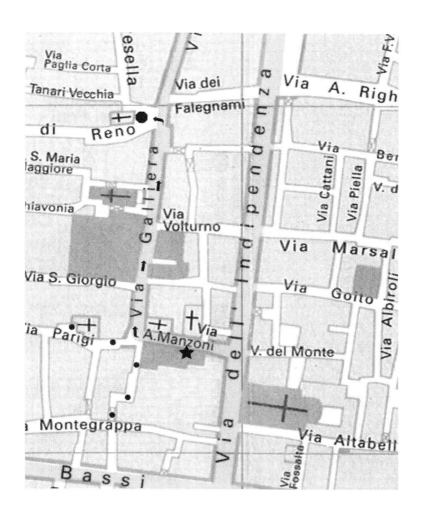

Map for *Fragments*

Figure 22. Via Galliera, Detail of Porticato

A Charming Interlude

I entered under the portico through doors thrown wide open and was surprised to find two men working at desks behind a wooden railing. I had expected to find a charming chapel in the small edifice I had noticed while wandering through the neighborhood. Vivid frescoes of the Last Judgment and Hell, among other dark, serious subjects, decorated the lunettes under the portico and beckoned, hinting at surprises within. The building had been the ex-church of the Madonna dell'Orazione (also San Colombano) and was built in 1591 by order of Pope Gregory XIII. The deconsecrated church now houses Bologna's Disabled Veterans Association (Via Parigi 1) along with a wealth of art from the fourteenth century to early seventeenth century.

An elderly gentleman on the phone motioned that he would be with me in a moment. The other one was busy at his desk with a client who was clearly impatient with the bureaucracy's machinations.

I glanced around the small receiving area at walls covered with frescoes and paintings. A lovely fresco of the Madonna feeding the baby Christ as he looks out to embrace the world formed a centerpiece on the wall facing the entrance. The juxtaposition of bureaucratic military with religious art startled me. The fresco is by Lippo di Dalmasio (1352–1410), the grandson of Simone de' Crocifissi.

Bologna Reflections

After nearly ten minutes, the gentleman, having finished his phone conversation, approached me, limping slightly. "Buon giorno, signora," he said with a smile and extended hand. "Can I help you?" he added, his smile widening to reassure me. "Are you here to see our marvelous frescoes? I suspect so," he said, without waiting for my response. He lifted his flat, brown, tweed cap courteously with his right hand, tipped his head slightly, scratched his forehead with a couple of fingers, and replaced the cap.

"Sì, signore," I responded. He obviously understood Italian was not my mother tongue, and I was relieved not to have to beg or explain my purpose.

It was clear that he liked the tour guide aspect of his work, which I later learned he performed as a volunteer. He smiled, reached for the keys, and informed his colleague that the signora needed a guide. Then he turned back to me. "It would be a pleasure to show you, signora," he said. "I am Alberto Veronesi, and Bologna is my beautiful city. Thank you for coming."

Surprised by the enthusiastic welcome, I managed to introduce myself and describe my mission: uncovering some of the hidden treasures of his city. He steered me toward the side doorway. We chatted as we walked past Dalmasio's Madonna. He nodded, as if greeting the Mother and Child, and said "See, everywhere one looks there is art." He liked the art's company and enjoyed sharing it with others, especially foreigners who manage to stumble upon the place.

As he led me through a side door into a hallway and up the stairs to the oratorio, he talked about his city and the wonders about which the Bolognesi themselves know nothing. "How did you find us here, signora?" he ventured. "See, even a foreigner finds us when the Bolognesi don't even try."

Trying to take the burden off the poor Bolognesi, I insisted, "It is normal not to notice the beauty in one's own city. Life intrudes, Signor Veronesi, don't you believe that, too?"

"Sì, sì," he agreed readily, "but it is a shame not to appreciate what is nearby."

Darkness greeted us when we entered the spacious oratorio. My guide explained that the drapes were usually kept closed to protect the valuable frescoes from the damaging sunlight. As he opened them, he described the scene that would have greeted a visitor to the oratorio in the year 1600.

"Signora, imagine it if you can, a stable of young artists, full of energy and ideas, with dreams of fame, and anxious to create something beautiful and inspiring in this place of prayer!" He explained that students of the renowned Carracci family of artists had been given the task of decorating the oratorio's walls. "What a competition it must have been," he added, laughing, "with each young man trying to out-do the other and grab the attention of the Master— and perhaps God's, too."

"Yes, I see, but who were they? And . . ."

He jumped right in before I could finish my question and said, "Look here, look here, Signora . . . look at the lively movement and obvious emotion up above us!"

I kept staring, unable to focus very well because he kept moving on, eager to show me another wall and another young artist's work: Domenichino (age 19); Lorenzo Garbieri (20); Francesco Albani (22); Galanino (23); Guido Reni and Francesco Brizio (25); and Lucio Massari (31).

When he had finished, I went back to the beginning and, moving slowly from one wall to the other, tried to feel their youth and absorb their message. The dim room and the age-darkened colors made the process difficult.

Bologna Reflections

The cycle is called *Episodi della vita di Cristo* (*Episodes in the Life of Christ*) and they represent his passion and death. For centuries no one knew who authored the cycle. Recently it was attributed to the famous school of the Carracci in Bologna during the late sixteenth and early seventeenth centuries, the young men my guide had mentioned.

The frescoes were all executed around the year 1600 and each panel contains the work of one of the young artists.

I went from one window to the next with Signor Veronesi as he shut the drapes and continued to discuss the frescoes and the artists. Then he moved on to the beauty of Bologna's streets and palazzi and—

"Signora," he began again, "will you return?" "Yes," I reassured him. "And I'll tell others about this hidden place too."

"Brava, brava, signora," he chuckled, "and now, while we walk downstairs I want you to tell me everything about your family and your city!"

~

That was in May 1995. I returned to the oratorio in March 2001. The frescoes had been restored. Signor Veronesi was still volunteering his services in the much-altered reception area of the Associazione Mutilati e Invalidi di Guerra. Again he was my guide, and again his enthusiasm and knowledge were at least as wonderful as the frescoes. Now, with their colors vibrantly alive, they seem to spring from the walls and tell the stories of the young artists, as artists and as men. The original wood ceiling, decorated with the shields of the various guilds that funded the sixteenth century oratorio, has also been rescued from the darkness. As a postscript to the earlier story I add that Signor Veronesi could not chat at length. A group of Bolognesi was forming to enjoy one of his personally guided tours.

138

Episodes in the Life of Christ

    I. *Il pianto di San Pietro* (*The Tears of St. Peter*) by Francesco Albani (1578–1660).

    II. *La Flagellazione* (*The Flagellation*) probably by Domenichino (1581–1641).

    III. *La Coronazione di spine* (*The Crowning with Thorns*) by Guido Reni (1575–1642).

    IV. *L'andata al Calvario* (*The Way of the Cross*) by Francesco Brizio (1574–1625).

    V. *Gesù inchiodato sulla Croce* (*Christ Nailed to the Cross*) by Lucio Massari (1569–1633).

    VI. *Il compianto sopra il Cristo deposto* (*The Mourning over the Body of Christ*) by Lorenzo Garbieri (1580–1654).

    VII. *Il trionfo di Cristo* (*The Triumph of Christ*) by Galanino (1577–1638).

    VIII. *La discesa di Cristo al Limbo* (*Christ's Descent into Purgatory*) by Domenichino.

    XI. *L'Angelo che batte il demonio* (*The Angel Beating the Devil*) by Galanino.

    X. *La deposizione nel Sepolcro* (*The Deposition of Christ's Body in the Tomb*) by Domenichino.

    XI. *L'orazione nell'orto* (*The Praying in the Garden*) by Guido Reni.

Figure 23. Canale del Reno, *Doing the Laundry* with Street Side Reflection

Voices of the Past

S tanding today at the Grada, where Via della Grada intersects the viale at Via Sabotino, I call up images of Bologna as a city of water, boats, and bridges. The church of Santa Maria and San Valentino della Grada was up against the city's third set of city walls. Next to it, a squat fourteenth century torrione still marks the entrance of the Canale del Reno into the city. "Grada" refers to the two black metal grates that hang on bulky chains attached to the side of the tower and cover the entrance of the canal. The water can sit green and stagnant at the tower or charge ferociously under it into the city. The grates are ready to drop—clank!—to protect Bologna from an invasion. Merciless, the sharp pointed teeth would have pierced anyone trying to enter unannounced and unwelcome. In fact, the Grada provided the ancient city with a variety of defensive possibilities. One rainy night in 1507, when French troops were camping in the plain ready to attack Bologna, the city closed the water gate and caused the fields to flood. The French had to retreat.

I follow the course of the Canale del Reno as it once flowed through the city, supplying the silk mills with power and, at times, the people with a place to wash their clothes or take a dip to cool off in the hot, humid summer. Old photographs show the banks near the Grada lined with washer women, white scarves wrapped around their heads, wet clothing stretched out on the tiers of concrete, stones, or bricks to dry in the sun. Only the rich palazzi had indoor washing facilities. They labored in the summer and the winter, in all kinds of weather. Other photos show laughing youngsters splashing in the canal's water on hot summer days.

When the Canale del Reno was still uncovered, the Ponte della Carità (Bridge of Charity), at the intersection of Via San Felice and Via della Grada, once played an integral role in the daily life of the neighborhood. A crowded meeting place, official city announcements were read out loud while people socialized and transacted business. The bridge was notorious because individuals often met their end by either jumping in voluntarily or by being pushed in maliciously. Other persons could then earn a bit of cash by saving them from the canal's turbulent water.

I follow Via Riva di Reno to its intersection with Via delle Lame, approaching the church of the Madonna del Ponte (Madonna of the Bridge) from the rear. The sixteenth century structure sticks up from the middle of the street today, just as it once rose up from the canal. Even on a modern map the topology of this street evokes a sense of its former life, the gentle turn suggesting the waterway that still flows underneath.

Via Abbadia is narrow and twists and turns its way from Via Riva di Reno to Via San Felice. The Ponte della Badia, one of Bologna's most evocative bridges, once arched over the graceful bend of the canal here. Where Via Abbadia angles toward Via San Felice, a military hospital replaces what used to be the ancient abbey of Saints Naborre and Felice. A fourteenth century bell tower and cloister remain. According to legend, St. Zama erected the first cathedral in Bologna in this location in 270AD. Evidence suggests that the complex's twelfth century crypt used the older material in its construction.

At the very end of the little street, where it meets busy Via San Felice, a charming shrine to the Madonna ornaments the wall of the palazzo on the left.

142

Although dark and grimy from the passing of time and traffic, it is adorned by a sprig of flowers. The blues and reds still show through the soot as well as the young mother's soft smile and the queen's crown on her head. The words "Ave Maria" are posted above her. Like the Madonna and the ancient abbey, veiled with layers of history in the almost irrelevant modern street, Bologna's hidden waterways tell stories of her past.

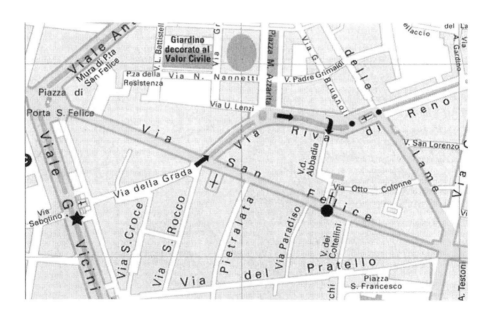

Map for *Voices of the Past*

Figure 24. Under the Portico, Study

The Ancient University

Figure 25. Tomb of Rolandino dei Romanzi, Study

146

The University of Bologna: Alma Mater Studiorum

No, no, no, this is not what I imagined, I mumbled. I had found the Palazzo dell'Università (Via Zamboni 33) but it hardly evoked the image of the Alma Mater Studiorum, the "Glorious Mother of Learning," the first university of the Western World. As a visitor to Bologna, my heart yearned more toward a romantic glimpse into the soul of a medieval city.

The presence of the Antico Studio (the ancient university) has been a crucial thread in the richly textured tapestry of Bologna's history since the eleventh century, weaving in and out resolutely, despite the continuous conflicts between Church, Empire, and Comune for control. Via Zamboni, the present center of the venerable institution where I began my search, has been part of its history since about 1803 when Napoleon designated the palazzi the university's home. At the same time he changed it from a church-governed organization to the state one it remains today.

Next my mind jumped to the Palazzo dell'Archiginnasio (Piazza Galvani 1). All university lectures finally took place under one roof at its inauguration in 1563, when it was called Palazzo delle Scuole Nuove by the

Roman Catholic Church, which had taken over university control. A remarkable edifice, yes, but not the seat of the original university.

In fact, the Antico Studio did not exist in any building. No documented evidence proves its origins. Even the date 1088, the usual one parlayed about, is questionable. It was founded by order of no authority. Rather, the university was the flicker of an idea that found its early expression in Bologna because of various economic, social, and political contingencies of the time.

With the fall of the Western Roman Empire (476 AD), the manuscripts recording the laws that had governed the Roman Empire were removed to Ravenna, the new capital of the Eastern Roman Empire, and gathered together by Emperor Justinian into the *Corpus Iuris Civilis*. How the *Corpus Iuris Civilis* ended up in Bologna is not clear. Some speculate that during the eleventh century the Countess Matilde di Canossa played a role, given her involvement in the politics of the Holy Roman Empire and the Roman Catholic papacy, and her association with Irnerio, one of the nascent university's first luminaries.

Records from the eleventh century verify that certain Doctors of the law were teaching in Bologna, even though they do not show the presence of an organized school. The University of Bologna actually grew up around those great figures that studied, illuminated, and practiced Roman law as codified by Justinian. Three names are usually associated with its origins: Pepo, Graziano, and Irnerio. Historical evidence suggests that Pepo was teaching publicly in 1078 and could have been Irnerio's teacher. Irnerio and Graziano and their followers, known as *glossatori*, explained the Civil and Ecclesiastical Law respectively and, from those famous glosses, or comments, written in the manuscripts' margins, the Alma Mater Studiorum's critical thread began to weave in and out of Bologna's history.

148

Why was the study of law important in the early eleventh century? And why did it happen in Bologna? The threat of barbaric invasions had diminished and, consequently, commerce grew in the Pianura Padana. Commercial activity required laws to regulate it. Roman rather than Germanic Law suited the structure of the emerging cities and their commerce. Bologna's central location on the Via Emilia, between Rimini (the Adriatic Sea) and Piacenza (toward the West), made the city a transportation and commercial hub even then. Everyone was traveling it seemed—monks, merchants, adventurers, pilgrims, soldiers returning from the Crusades, and, eventually, students and professors, too.

Word spread rapidly that in hospitable Bologna one could study jurisprudence. The arrival of students and professors from all of Italy, and from much of Europe, caused a crisis in the relatively small walled city. The predominantly rich foreign students and their servants needed housing, food, clothing, books, financial services, and entertainment. Therefore, other people came from the countryside, and sometimes from great distances, to take care of them: the artisans arrived to make the cloth and shoes; the merchants to sell their wares and services; the farmers to provide food, to name just a few. In other words, Bologna flourished. The city expanded within the second set of walls. The Cerchia del Mille, with its gates known as the *torresotti*, was completed in 1192. They opened up at both large and small roads and points where the waterways entered and exited the city. Then a third set of walls became necessary in the early thirteenth century.

The students were often young men, the rich sons of the emerging merchant class in Europe, who wished to climb the social ladder or whose families' businesses required expertise in the law. They were young noblemen interested in theology or ecclesiastical law—or adventure. They were also men 30 years and older, sometimes priests, sometimes not, pursuing studies in either ecclesiastical or civil law, or the liberal arts. Some perhaps even intended to prolong their freedom from family responsibilities by studying.

The life of a student was expensive, with as many, if not more, fees to be paid for tuition, books, gifts, and exams, than today's university students face. Then, too, the costs of clothing, shoes, and entertainment had to be figured in. Poor students could study because the church or rich patrons wanting religious indulgences gave them scholarships. Of course, their lives would have been much less extravagant.

Women also earned degrees and taught at the Alma Mater Studiorum because ancient laws enacted in Bologna allowed it: Clotilde Tambroni, Laura Bassi, and Anna Mazzolini are examples. In fact, according to historical accounts, Novella, the daughter of Giovanni D'Andrea, an important jurist, took over his university position at his death in 1348. However, because she was so lovely, a protective screen placed between her and the students prevented her beauty from distracting them as she lectured.

Just a few of the University of Bologna's famous students and professors of the past and present have been Dante Alighieri, Francesco Petrarca, Giovanni Boccaccio, Nicolas Copernicus, Pier Paolo Pasolini, and Umberto Eco, whose lectures one might catch today.

Those who studied with the earliest doctors of the law and passed the required exams were then qualified to teach. Therefore, the activities of the university continued to grow in Bologna, in other Italian cities, and in Europe. Positions became plentiful and professors a traveling crowd. Eventually, Bologna made it illegal for professors to leave to teach elsewhere because the good professors were departing to take advantage of prospects elsewhere.

The privileges, like the positions, were sought by everyone. In medieval Bologna, a student would greet his professor as *meus dominus* (my lord). His career brought the professor fame, prestige, good earnings, and respect. The number of his students equaled the level of respect accorded him—and the level of his earnings. Positions became so coveted that Giovanni D'Andrea declared that, at his death, his descendents would inherit his seat.

The professors, together with a group of students, paid homage to Emperor Federico Barbarosa who camped near the Reno River on his way to Rome in 1154. As the result of the meeting and their discussion, the Emperor issued a document called *Autentica Habita* in which he conceded various privileges and protections to the university community in Bologna.

The fame of the city as a center for judicial studies caused crowded conditions, which, in turn, resulted in problems for the students. They needed help especially in locating lodging and procuring a qualified teacher. Because the Comune realized that Bologna's booming economy depended on a healthy university population, it often enacted laws to protect the students and professors and to favor their status in the community. Some of the statutes assured that foreign students and professors were granted citizenship, with all the rights that implied: the houses in which they lived could not be destroyed for any reason, noise was prohibited near houses where they lived or studied, and they could buy unlimited grain and not be overcharged.

At first the professors would come to Bologna for a couple of years and then move on, making for a very lively cultural exchange. However, in the middle of the fourteenth century, the Comune took control of the university because fierce competition from universities in other cities threatened Bologna's hegemony. When that political body instead of the students began to select and pay the professors and impose innumerable requisites and restrictions, the Studio lost some of its original vitality.

Bologna Reflections

During the Middle Ages the bells of the churches and monasteries regulated the rhythm of everyday life, the daytime and nighttime hours, divided into twelve fractional parts. Depending on the season, the amount of available sunlight would vary. The lives of the professors and students depended on the number of daylight hours, so their day began early.

The student, like almost every other citizen, would normally get up about five a.m., dress in the customary outfit befitting his rank and duty, wash his hands and maybe his face, attend Mass at six, and eat a breakfast of bread and watered-down wine.

The long school year went from the tenth of October until the end of August, with vacations interspersed throughout. The school day began officially at nine a.m. when the bell from San Pietro would announce the commencement of the *ordinaria*, the lesson that presented the day's new material. The professors began their lectures as soon as the church bell rang. The students sat on their benches, the teacher at the front, where a table held the large volume about which he would comment. At noon they ate the midday meal, followed by two hours of debate. From three until five p.m. another lesson, the *straordinaria*, went into more depth on a topic already studied. At the end of the afternoon lesson, the evening meal of bread and soup would follow. A quick in-between snack of biscuits, a wedge of cake, or a cheese or meat pie from a convenient bakery was always in the offing. Then in the evening Bologna's many osterie—locales where students could drink, eat, play a game or two of cards, fight, and womanize—offered obvious possibilities. Of course, the good students and professors would be home studying, until their candles burned too low, and then in bed early.

Initially, the rapport between professors and students was a very personal one. The students organized themselves, chose a professor, and paid for his services, attending lessons for a year. In the thirteenth century the

152

professors gave lessons in their own houses or in nearby rented quarters. The students also paid the rent and the cost of furnishing the teaching space. They paid tuition to the professor and rented their seats, even though they also paid the rent!

When the student finished his course of studies, he took an exam, called first the *licentia* and later in the thirteenth century the *laurea*. He paid a very high fee to take the exam and also had to regal the professor with expensive gifts.

As early as the end of the twelfth century the students formed into a society called Universitas Scholarium, which was actually a corporation or union meant to look out for their privileges and rights. They were further divided into groups of Italian students (Universitas Citramontanarum) and foreign students (Universitas Ultramontanarum). At the head of each group was a rector, chosen from among the richest students, who had many obligations in representing them. The rectors were assisted by a council of thirty-eight members and together would choose the professors, oversee enrollment, deal with the rental of student houses from the Comune, work out details with those that copied the manuscripts, and control the production and availability of books.

Toward the end of the thirteenth century, the number of students having increased dramatically, they divided themselves into groups according to faculty, and took over various neighborhoods of the city. For instance, the law school gathered in the neighborhood within the streets of Via San Mamolo, Via dei Libri (Via Farini), Corte dei Bulgari (where the Palazzo dell'Archiginnasio was eventually built), Guasto degli Andolò (Via Farini, 2–6), Via delle Casette di Sant'Andrea (Via Garibaldi, near Piazza Cavour), and the Porta San Procolo (near the church of San Paolo Maggiore). The school of medicine and the arts assembled in the neighborhood of Piazza San Salvatore to the Porta Nova, to Via delle Banzole (across from the west side of today's Palazzo Comunale), to the church of San Francesco. Evidently, the Comune of Bologna encouraged the separation to help stem the raucous, sometimes bloody confrontations that took place between the students of the two faculties.

From the last years of the thirteenth century until the sixteenth century, the lively Antico Studio di Bologna could be found in those specific neighborhoods, not in Via Zamboni. Meandering in their old, dark, narrow streets today still evokes the mood and penetrates the soul of the Alma Mater Studiorum.

Figure 26. Vaults, Study

The Palazzo dell'Archiginnasio

The courtyard of the Palazzo dell'Archiginnasio is quiet, with long shafts of morning sunlight cutting through the shadows thrown by its graceful arches and elegant double loggia. A few people enter with me, their destination, no doubt, the famous library on the upper floor or the Teatro Anatomico (Theater of Anatomy). Many visitors to Bologna search for the Alma Mater Studiorum, the ancient university, in this edifice. Although they do not find the institution's earliest beginnings here, the story of the palazzo and the university is an old one, going back to the sixteenth century.

Bologna became a Papal State at the tumultuous end of the Bentivoglio family's rule in 1506. The Church also took control of the university. It refused to honor the jurisdiction of the rectors and the privileges that the professors and students had previously been granted by the Comune. Consequently, as they hastened off to other institutions in Italy, the university's prestige declined.

In 1561, to rekindle interest in Bologna's university and house all of its activities under one roof, representatives of the Roman Catholic Church ordered the construction of the Archiginnasio. Wanting to flaunt its power during that time of the Counter-Reformation, the Church also wanted more rigid control over the exchange of ideas. The structure was erected in seventeen months, from spring 1562 to autumn 1563, under the direction of architect Antonio Morandi, also called il Terribilia.

Bologna Reflections

Today silence and decorum often reign, but back then the Archiginnasio's courtyard would have been filled with the hustle and bustle of students and professors in their black flowing robes. Crowds of law students would have climbed the wide stairs on the right to their classrooms on the second floor, while the students of the liberal arts would head toward their own *aule* (classrooms) using the stairway to the left.

A plethora of heraldic shields hanging under arches, around corridors, over stairways, and in the halls gives a sense of Bologna as the center of the world during those early centuries. History reveals itself in every shade of blue and red, gold, black, and white; in fits of circles and squares; in fantastic winged dragons and griffins; in swirls of flowers, stodgy trees, braying horses, and formidable castles and towers. Names of cities, regions, countries force me to imagine traveling to corners of the then distant world: Polonia, Florentia, Neapoli, Palermo, Alamania, Ungaria, Cypro, Sicilia, Venetia, Anglia, Austria, Catalonia, Portugalia, Frantia, Burgundia, Flandria, Feraria, Valentia, Prusia, Ispania, Apulia, Scotia. Even the first American, Diego de Leon Garavito from Lima, Peru, is remembered as a university prior in 1607.

Since the sixteenth century the Palazzo dell'Archiginnasio has also been the venue for some of Bologna's most captivating spectacles.

In the grandstand of the Teatro Anatomico upstairs, I sit opposite the throne-like *cattedra* (desk) of the professor, whose wooden canopy is held up elegantly by the two, linden wood *spellati* (persons without skin) of Ercole Lelli (1735). The cedar and pine interior, designed by Antonio Levanti (1638–49), suggests warmth, more so today because the bright sun enters from the windows on the east. The linden statues in the niches (sculpted by Silvestro Giannotti) and I are the only audience to the imagined goings on in the grand anatomical theater of long ago.

158

Already in the thirteenth century some dissection of cadavers and autopsies had been performed for legal and medical reasons. Mondino de' Liuzzi, the great anatomist, lectured publicly in Bologna from 1314 to 1324. He was the first to treat anatomy as a separate science in the study of medicine but faced obstacles because his contemporaries placed blind faith in the writings of Galeno (129–201 AD), a Roman doctor, physiologist, and anatomist from Pergamo in Asia Minor. In addition, laws had been enacted that forbade the procedures.

Ultimately Mondino's work triumphed and for three centuries medical students used his textbook *Anatomia* to study the human body and the techniques for performing autopsies. In 1315, perhaps with his assistant Alessandra Ziliani da Persicito, he held the first public lesson of anatomy using parts of the human body. The principles of anatomy professed by Mondino had a strong following from the 1500s and eventually the Roman Catholic Church accepted them in the eighteenth century. Then the Archiginnasio's Teatro Anatomico became the arena for the ritual.

Imagining the spectacle certainly makes history entertaining. The Academy of Doctors performed the dissections in winter because of difficulty preserving cadavers, which were not easy to acquire either. Sometimes they were even stolen from graves or taken down, still swinging, immediately following a public hanging in Piazza Maggiore. After the feast of St. Anthony the Abbot (January 17), during the long winter vacation, the dissections were held for ten continuous mornings and afternoons. Grandly ceremonial, the spectacles were attended by official representatives of the State, the Church, the University, and by common priests and lowly citizens. Even women of the nobility would attend out of curiosity. If the period came during Carnevale, persons in masks would join the crowd, adding a macabre atmosphere to the solemn occasion.

Bologna Reflections

The Teatro Anatomico was hung with rich draperies. Plushy-rich damask and velvet cushions rested on the hard wooden seats. The position of honor, the slab of white marble front and center, belonged to the cadaver.

Meanwhile, the illustrious professor, red robes puffed up around him sat, *in cattedra*, at the desk above the dissection, the pertinent giant textbook spread open before him. He read the text and gave directions to the dissector. The lecturer was assisted by the *ostensore*, who indicated with a long pointer, the step-by-step procedure: first the stomach, then the chest, then the other parts of the body, and lastly the head.

Before the beginning of the dissection the professor and all of his assistants attended a Mass, offered up, of course, for the person whose body they would dissect. The doctor's obligations included giving the Church about four pounds of wax for candles, and paying all costs for draping the Teatro, for the torches, etc. For a first dissection he must also add, as a sign of homage to the chief doctor, eight candles of white Venetian wax, two portions of sugar, a pair of costly gloves from Rome, and a fine majolica platter, suitable for serving a pleasantly plump capon.

But that was not all. Designated students from time to time interrupted, often dramatically, and criticized the procedure. In addition, a small, high window still exists today on the north wall from which an unknown *contraddittore* (contradictor), protected from view by a fine grate, called out accusatory and provocative questions to the professor. The adversary was usually a representative of the Catholic Church, bringing into question the contradictions of science in the interest of religion. The professor had to have a calm temperament to avoid becoming flustered by the unexpected opening of the window from on high, and the sudden critical, often philosophical, questions that rained down from the voice above. The window eventually closed, just as unexpectedly, and the teaching professor continued his ceremonious work while the dutiful audience watched the spectacle.

Downstairs in the courtyard another command performance played out as the city's *Teriaca* was brewed in the month of August from the sixteenth century until the end of the eighteenth century. An air of excitement surrounded the busy pharmacists and doctors assembling the sixty or so ingredients necessary to create the city's official medicinal remedy for almost every existing infirmity, including the plague. Teriaca is the name given by Galeno to the antidotes against bites of venomous animals. His was the first recipe to include, along with a variety of other vegetable substances, the flesh of snakes. The ideal aging process for the brew was said to be twelve years, and one ingested it mixed with either water or wine.

In the Middle Ages, the concoction was made in pharmacies. Then in the second half of the sixteenth century, the pharmacists came together to produce it at convents. That of San Salvatore became one of the important centers. Finally, perhaps to bestow even more prestige on its preparation, the officials convened in the courtyard of the Palazzo dell'Archiginnasio, and a popular festival evolved. The pharmacists and doctors fixed the date to begin and assembled the ingredients, which were exhibited first to the public for three days. Richly ornamented curtains draped the sides of the courtyard, and two pyramidal shelves held the busts of Hypocrites and Galeno. Majolica vases lined up patiently, waiting to hold the remedy. Doctors, scholars, ordinary citizens, nobles, everyone came. The preparation took three months. Under the protection of a broad, decorated canopy, huge cauldrons smoked, while a number of tables were mounted with distilling paraphernalia, mortars, filters, and every sort of instrument used by doctors and pharmacists. A large group of assistants, their uniforms suitably ornate, helped the officials in charge.

Bologna Reflections

After the Teriaca had been assembled, cooked, and cooled, it was put in the medicinal majolica urns and distributed to the city's pharmacies. It was prescribed for many illnesses: fever, cough, arthritis, melancholy, late and irregular menstrual cycles, and the plague, during which time it was given out liberally. Did it work? With such an extensive list of ingredients, some effect had to have been felt for some of the conditions.

Those are spectacles of the past, but the Palazzo dell'Archiginnasio's history continues today. Sometimes on a summer evening the same courtyard, forever a focal point of culture and public life in Bologna, is filled with the strains of lilting music or animated voices discussing history or art. I, too, become part of that life while wandering through, both imagining the echoes of its past and enjoying the magic of the today.

The Palazzo dell'Archiginnasio

Figure 27. Palazzo Pepoli, Via Castiglione 4–8

Secrets Around the Corner

Via D'Azeglio is Bologna's chic parlor, a focal point in the city's social life. Walk down its length in order to "be seen," enjoy a *caffè* or *aperitivo* (aperitif) at one of its pleasant street side bars, or shop in its stylish boutiques. The absence of cars and motorini allows quiet conversation. And then, too, there is the past to consider. The street leads into an old quarter of narrow lanes and little piazzas, and around every corner another neighborhood secret waits to be discovered: medieval house towers, warring families, bordellos, a Roman theater, chocolate, the ancient university, beloved Madonnas, and even a love story.

Step into the miniature Corte de' Galuzzi, just off of Via D'Azeglio and you'll find yourself transported back into medieval Bologna. Shades of the city's characteristic red colors the piazzetta, from the dirty reddish-brown of the tower's small bricks to the red and peach ocher stucco that stain the nearby palazzi. The Galuzzi family's tower, once much taller than its present 98 feet, was built in 1257. The Galuzzi family's realm extended beyond the piazza itself. In 1369 Antonio Galuzzi erected Santa Maria Rotonda dei Galuzzi and the Oratorio San Giovanni Battista di Fiorentini in the courtyard, toward Via D'Azeglio.

The Galuzzi family conducted ferocious feuds with their powerful rivals from their piazza headquarters. In the second half of the thirteenth century Bologna's principal families usually fit into one of two factions: the Guelfs, loyal to the Papacy, and the Ghibillines, faithful to the Empire. The Galuzzi belonged to the Guelf party.

Bologna's very own legend of star-crossed lovers, a story full of treachery, intrigue, and love, was a result of those Galluzzi feuds. Virginia Galluzzi fell in love with Alberto Carbonesi, whose family belonged to the Ghibelline faction. When the young woman's father Giampietro discovered that the couple had been secretly married, he killed Alberto, along with others who had aided the lovers. Virginia, desperate without Alberto, hung herself from the balcony of a Carbonesi house. As I walk on Via de' Carbonesi now, I imagine the tragic scene and the drama that unfolded. And in my version of the legend, the young and beautiful Romeo and Juliet from Franco Zeffirelli's 1968 film become Alberto and Virginia, impatient and full of passion.

Today the wars have stopped. The tower and neighboring palazzo on Via D'Azeglio is a complex of media store and modern bar, welcoming passersby to step inside.

This neighborhood was also a nucleus for the early university. Many students and professors took quarters here, and space was rented for lessons in the streets south and west of Via D'Azeglio. Another Galuzzi, Bonifacio, was an important doctor of ecclesiastical law in the mid-fourteenth century. On his tombstone, now housed in the Museo Civico Medievale, he is depicted at his desk, students grouped on either side. No one seems to be paying much attention: they whisper and read, and one monk looks as if he were praying.

On the west side of Via D'Azeglio stand the church of San Giovanni Battista dei Celestini and the former convent of the Celestine monks. The Archivio di Stato or State Archives are now housed here. The piazza in front of the church and ex-convent narrows to tiny Vicolo Santo Spirito, once called

Borgo del Bordello because prostitutes used to call out from the windows of the thirteenth century Torrecasa dei Catalani to prospective clients below. The poor monks had to put up with the chaos—bickering between jealous prostitutes, bickering between prostitutes and their clients, downright fighting between raucous students—until 1520 when the city finally closed down the bordello.

According to tradition, there was a time in Bolognese history when prostitutes were confined to their closed houses and allowed to exit only once a week. In addition, they had to wear a large white sash embroidered with roses over their dresses while on the public street. Bells on the sash rang as the prostitute walked so that passersby would know to clear the way for the "sinner." If she ignored the law, her nose was cut off.

The quarter is also home to remains of Roman Bononia. In the 1980s the relics of the Roman theater were discovered in an area beneath today's Via de' Carbonesi, at the southernmost confines of the Roman city, revealing yet another secret of the past. A full semi-circle in shape, about 246 feet in diameter, the theater opened to the north. Scholars believe it was constructed between 120 and 80 BC. Until the COIN department store relocated from Via de' Carbonesi to Via Rizzoli, it was possible to see the ruins of the theater underneath the Plexiglas floor of the store.

Bologna's sweet chocolate heart can also to be found in this neighborhood, next door to the vestiges of the ancient theater. I am a slave to the melt-in-your mouth cioccolatini created by Majani, available in a lovely little shop in Via de' Carbonesi 5/B. My favorite is the Fiat Cremino, a layered, dice-shaped chunk of chocolate, almond, and hazelnut cream.

Around the corner lies Via Val D'Aposa, named after a now dried-up canal that once entered Bologna here. The dollhouse-like Oratorio dello Spirito Santo (Via Val D'Aposa 6) adorns the narrow street, whose ordinary yellow and

167

rusty red palazzi have low, dark porticoes. The Celestine monks erected the oratorio from 1481 to 1497, and the delightful facade has intricate terracotta decorations that seem like blue and pink icing on a delectable milk chocolate cake. Stumbling upon it unexpectedly is like uncovering a sweet secreted away in the corner of someone else's pantry.

I head there now and, after pausing a moment to savor again the delight of the oratorio, I go south on Via Val D'Aposa away from the center. Hidden on Via Barberia, Palazzo Monti-Salina's secret is a quiet courtyard with a fourteenth century well created by the Dalle Masegne (Via Barberia 13). I duck inside the open portone and breathe in the quietness of the space, thinking of the gray, tired well and the life that has unfolded around it over the centuries— the idle gossip, secret trysts, and dangerous intrigues.

Back outside, giant buses, cars, and zooming motorini negotiate tortuous Via Barberia. Little food markets and antique stores mix in comfortably with several impressive palazzi. Suddenly the sidewalk and portico end at a shrine to the Madonna and Child (Palazzo Marescotti, Via Barberia 4). A graceful black wrought iron gate encloses the space under a fresco by Felice Pasqualini, *Madonna della notte e delle ombre* (*Madonna of the Night and the Shadows*). I find it natural to stop for a moment. The simple masses of fresh flowers and plants that always adorn the spot intimate that someone tends the shrine with devotion.

Then at nearby Piazza di San Paolo Maggiore, a number of clues suggest the importance of the intersection in Bologna's history. A sign with a white cross in a field of red stained glass swings from a black wrought iron hanger above a modern pharmacy's entrance (Via Collegio di Spagna 1). The plaque under it explains that the Antica Spezieria (an early pharmacy), founded in the fourteenth century, once occupied the space at the "sign of the pinecone." I wonder if colorful majolica vases of Teriaca were once brought

168

here from the Palazzo dell'Archiginnasio to be dispensed in the neighborhood. Next to it on the wall is a medallion with an inscription that says:

> Here was the cross of the Saints, as decreed by St. Ambrose, bishop of Milan, in the year 393 and transferred in 1798 to San Petronio by Cardinal Andrea Gioanetti, to protect it from the violence of the French Revolution.

When Sant'Ambrogio came to Bologna in the early fourth century, the city was in shambles from barbaric invasions. According to legend, he urged the bishop Petronio to place four crosses around the edges of the ruined city, creating a symbolic wall of protection for the people. *La Croce dei Santi* (Cross of the Saints) was here where ancient Porta San Procolo controlled entrance into the city. He positioned *La Croce dei Martiri* (Cross of the Martyrs) at Porta Castello, today's Via Montegrappa. *La Croce degli Apostoli ed Evangelisti* (Cross of the Apostles and Evangelists) was at Porta Ravegnana and *La Croce delle Vergini* (Cross of the Virgins) at the intersection of Via Castiglione and Via Farini. Now the originals are in the basilica of San Petronio.

From Piazza di San Paolo Maggiore, Via Collegio di Spagna curves gently toward its eventual intersection with Via Saragozza. It is named for the complex that fills the triangular block and has connected it to the history of Bologna's university. Cardinal Egidio Albornoz, Archbishop of Toledo, constructed the Collegio di Spagna in the fourteenth century to host twenty-four Spanish students of noble birth while they attended the Università di Bologna. The building, constructed in the 1360s, is still Spanish property and continues to house visiting Spanish students. A crenellated wall surrounds the compound, which also includes the church of San Clemente Martiro, a courtyard with a double loggia and a tranquil garden. The library is rich in rare editions and maintains an impressive archive of the institution's entire history.

Bologna Reflections

Whenever I find myself at the point where Via Collegio di Spagna ends at Via Saragozza, I remember my first visit to Bologna and the wonderful afternoon when the Madonna di San Luca was carried down from the Colle della Guardia and the Bolognesi ushered her into the city center—and then I think about my own secret desire connected to the place.

~

Narrow Via Saragozza could not contain the crowd that was gathering at the Arco del Meloncello that Saturday afternoon in late May. We were all waiting for the descent of the Madonna from her sanctuary at the top of the Colle della Guardia (Hill of the Watch). Borne aloft on a flower-bedecked platform, the icon would be accompanied by a procession to the cathedral of San Pietro, where it would remain for a week of festivities in its honor.

This traditional Bolognese celebration honors an image of the Madonna and Child, which legend describes as one of those executed by San Luca (St. Luke) the Evangelist. It says that a Greek monk in the church of Santa Sofia in Constantinople discovered the Bolognese icon and was told to transport it to the Monte della Guardia. In Roma he learned by chance from a Bolognese official that the Monte della Guardia was in Bologna, and he delivered it there in 1160. Analysis shows that the representation was probably repainted in the twelfth century.

On that particular afternoon in 1994, the sky was blue and cloudless and the temperature warm, a perfect spring day to welcome the representation of the Madonna into the heart of the city. I was there as a spectator, to experience a Bolognese tradition. The crowd consisted of elderly signoras, young families with babies in strollers, and many extended families, including grandparents and cousins. A sense of anticipation electrified the air as friends and family members shouted greetings to each other and chatted excitedly. I felt part of the throng as we waited, even though I was alone.

Then a hush took over and absolute quiet settled on the gathering. The image of the Madonna had descended her hill, ready to be accompanied to the cathedral by her faithful. The Archbishop, priests, and religious clergy headed the pageant. One of the priests near the front of the procession led the crowd in saying the rosary. With great solemnity we moved slowly toward Porta Saragozza. Wildly ringing bells welcomed the procession each time it stopped at one of the churches along the way. People leaned out over windowsills decorated with flapping lengths of red cloth to wave and throw rose petals out over the parade as it passed.

Prayer, bells, and rose petals accompanied us as we squeezed through along the narrow streets. Our route went up Via Saragozza to Via Collegio di Spagna then followed Via de' Carbonesi and Via D'Azeglio right into Piazza Maggiore. All the church bells of the center rang as we entered the piazza and the icon and her cortege went off to the cathedral of San Pietro in Via dell'Indipendenza.

During the following week the bells of Bologna's churches pealed every evening at six to honor the statue's return to the city. Special masses and blessings were said in celebration of its presence. The cover was lifted from the *Madonna della Nicchia* on the facade of Palazzo Strazzaroli in Piazza di Porta Ravegnana, street side stalls sold candy and gifts, and a general carnival atmosphere prevailed in the city center. I had been surprised at the spirituality and silence during the procession on that Saturday afternoon and, later, at the joy that took over the piazzas for a week.

~

Bologna Reflections

That was one way to experience Via Saragozza, whose narrow porticoes snake along the street. Now it is time to reveal my own secret desire tied to the neighborhood: I have always wanted to live here. Why? The green hills are nearby. The colors of the palazzi and the porticoes—yellow, tangerine, papaya, orange, salmon, mango, tan, chestnut brown, gold, butternut, banana, and cantaloupe—make me hungry. The gardens back behind the portoni that face the street hide beauty and tranquility. The small stores and bars are neighborly, old, not spruced up into modern boutiques. Maybe someday, and then who knows what other secrets of the past I will discover there.

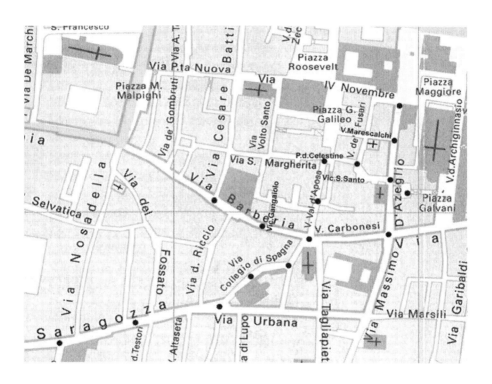

Map for *Secrets Around the Corner*

Figure 28. Oratorio dello Spirito Santo, Detail

Once Upon a Time in Bologna

River stones that recall a medieval past line Piazza San Domenico today. In the late eleventh century, however, just outside the city, vineyards covered the undulating, green hills that run south toward the Apennines. A few houses and a little church called the Oratorio di San Nicolò delle Vigne (Oratorio of St. Nicholas of the Vineyards) dotted this bit of land beyond the city wall of selenite, where today's piazza remains. Behind the place where the basilica of San Domenico now stands, the Torrente Aposa flowed north toward the center of Bologna, irrigating the fields in the countryside along the way. The park of Villa Ghigi, up Via San Mamolo past the Piazza di Porta San Mamolo, provides a great vantage point, surrounded by vineyards and orchards, from which to imagine Bologna "once upon a time"— the little country church, the river that no longer scurries out of the hills to the center, and the Alma Mater Studiorum, the ancient university tied so closely with this part of the city.

In March of 1219, after a group of Dominicans were given the church and the adjacent land, its leader Reginald of Orleans moved the small community here. They were followers of Domenico Guzman (1171–1221), the Spanish founder of their mendicant order. Their mission was to eradicate the heresies plaguing the Roman Catholic Church at the time, especially in the cities.

Bologna Reflections

San Domenico himself arrived in Bologna that same year and, before his death in 1221, he transformed it into an important center for the order. Since that time, the histories of the city and of San Domenico have been closely intertwined. He is considered one of its saint protectors, along with San Petronio, San Francesco d'Assisi, and San Procolo.

After Domenico's death, the church among vineyards became a destination for pilgrims. Work on a new complex began in 1228 because so many arrived to pray, to join the order, or to bury their dead near the saint. The edifice itself was finished in 1235 and eventually became the meeting place for the foreign law students crowding into the medieval city, taking the place of the nearby church of San Procolo. Many professors and students from the Università di Bologna also joined the order of preaching monks. The tombs of famous jurists, professors of the university, notaries, merchants, bankers, and members of noble families are in the basilica's Chiostro dei Morti (Cloister of the Dead).

On my first visit to Bologna, I was puzzled by two pyramidal structures that rise up above the stones in Piazza San Domenico. I assumed that they were memorials to famous warriors or princes but soon learned that Bologna's heroes have always been her Doctors of the Law. The monuments, in fact, honor two revered figures from the medieval university, Rolandino de' Passeggeri, an important notary and government official, and Egidio Foscherari, an expert in ecclesiastical law (1289). The carving on Rolandino's tomb (1305) remembers him as a teacher with students gathered around. Time has smoothed out its edges while it keeps watch in the piazza, but it remains a remarkable testimonial to the city's early history.

Four works of art draw me to visit the basilica time and again. Banks of red votive candles signal the large crucifix by Giunta Pisano (1250) on the wall just to the right of the main door. Farther along the right nave, harmony and

176

peace surround the white marble tomb of San Domenico, which shines out from the shadows of his chapel. A collection of artists created the memorial from the thirteenth century to the eighteenth century. In our world of quick results and fast turnover, it is difficult to imagine the patience of five centuries. From 1265 to 1267 Nicola Pisano worked with others to carve the saint's sarcophagus, which depicts scenes from San Domenico's life. Two hundred years later Nicolò dell'Arca (1469–73) added the magnificent marble crown, the *arca*, which is considered his capolavoro. He also executed the delicately graceful torch-bearing angel on the left side of the marble slab, with its serene, child-like face and tiny body swathed in a great, draping robe.

The young Michelangelo Buonarroti (1475–1564) created the angel holding the torch on the right, as well as the statues of San Petronio and San Procolo. His angel's gown does not mask the strong body underneath or the pent-up energy it contains. The young angel has been forced to hold still for an endless moment, but his mind is on flight, movement. With his athletic hulk, he looks like he would be out of place in the angel world. He peers out brashly, nothing demure about him.

Michelangelo's San Procolo and San Petronio, along with other figures, decorate the sides of the tomb. San Petronio (second from the left on the front) holds the city of Bologna in his hands, while the Roman soldier, Procolo, stands guard in the back with his sword.

Filippino Lippi's *Matrimonio Mistico di Santa Caterina* (*The Mystical Marriage of St. Catherine*, 1501) hangs in the chapel just to the right of the presbytery. The lightness and brightness of its colors, especially the red of St. Catherine's flowing gown, glows in the grayness of the immense church.

Finally, I step behind the main altar to the exquisite *coro* (choir) by the monk Damiano da Bergamo (1528–51). The choir consists of stalls formed by

177

separate panels of inlaid wood, delicately expressive and complex. Scenes from the Old and New Testament allow a glimpse inside the heart and soul of the monk. Drama and action fill the rectangles. With tiny slivers of wood, in tones that range from black to limpid beige and even silver, living, breathing Madonnas, saints, and townspeople inhabit perfectly crafted houses and walled castles. I see ducks float serenely down the stream and Santo Stefano being stoned to death. Flowers pop up in front of the birth of Christ in the stable and skies seem to move as the wind blows away the clouds. God the Father looks down from the heavens, while people peer out of earthbound windows at the flagellation of Christ. Patient Damiano's vision, crafted with fingers and eyes that must have grown exhausted from the tedious work, pulls me in. I move slowly from panel to panel, absorbing the glorious gift he has left us.

Leaving Damiano and Domenico's world behind, I roam in the neighborhood, which even now, almost a thousand years later, still resonates with the presence of jurisprudence in Bologna. The Palazzo di Giustizia (courthouse) dominates the nearby Piazza del Tribunale. Attorneys, their clients, and law students come and go, filling hectic bars and copy shops, while bookstores advertise law manuals, pamphlets, and texts in display windows.

The church of San Procolo (Via D'Azeglio 52) retains traces of its former position as a gathering place for law students. A plaque on the outside wall celebrates the relationship of the Benedictine church and convent of San Procolo to the Alma Mater Studiorum:

> In this Benedictine church of San Procolo, the university of foreign scholars held their meetings in the thirteenth century.
>
> And here outside were once the tombs of Bulgaro and Martino whom, with Jacopo and Ugo, all four doctors of the Studio of Bologna, called in the year 1158 by Frederick I, known as

the Barbarosa, to the Diet of Roncaglia where
they rendered the famous decision regarding the
rights of the Empire and those of the city.

Frederick proclaimed his sovereignty in Italy at the Diet of Roncaglia
(1158), but calling Bulgaro, Martino, Jacopo, and Ugo, important professors of
the ancient university, to participate, demonstrates the institution's prestige even
then. With their knowledge of the law, they helped to delineate the rights of the
independent Italian *comuni* (city-states) and those of the Holy Roman Empire.

San Procolo was martyred during the reign of Diocletian (284–305) but
two diverse theories of his origin persist. In one, he is a Roman soldier from
Bologna who was beheaded after refusing to renounce his Christian faith.
Legend says that he then picked up his head and carried it under his arm to the
spot where he wished a shrine be built. In the second version, Procolo was a
Syrian bishop who lived in the sixth century and hid in Bologna to evade the
persecution of the Emperor Tortila. He was found and beheaded. As if to give
weight to both traditions, two bodies were found in the little chapel dedicated
to the saint in 1398. The saint is usually represented as a young Roman soldier
with a sword, as the statue by Michelangelo in the church of San Domenico
illustrates.

According to tradition, a church has stood on this site since the fourth
century. Documented evidence suggests that extensive work transformed the
building in 1384 and then again in 1536. Bologna's Benedictine monks at that
time devoted themselves to caring for the sick and from 1494 were known as
the Fathers of the Orphans because of their special dedication to them. The
nearby Oratorio dei Bastardini, once an orphanage, reflects that history.

Once upon a time this part of Bologna was full of both natural and
artificial waterways. The Canale di Savena and its companions served in the

transportation of people and goods and powered the waterwheels that provided energy to small enterprises, including paper making, metal working, and cloth dying. The names of the streets call to mind the history: Cartoleria (paper store), Cotelli (knives), Tovaglie (tablecloths), Arienti (silver), Tagliapietre (stonecutters), Orfeo (goldsmiths), Savanella (little Savena), and Oro (gold). The water from the Canale di Savena was initially directed into the city during the twelfth century to fill the moat that circled outside the Cerchia dei Mille for protection from enemies and to power the flour mills in the northern reaches of the city. From the fifteenth century until the mid-seventeenth century, the water was put to use for the production of cloth and paper as well. Bologna's economy depended on the system of canals.

Walking toward the center of Bologna on Via Garibaldi, under a canopy of magnolia trees, I imagine the ancient city and the street as it was known then, Via delle Cassette di Sant'Andrea, where the law students used to attend their lessons at the professors' quarters and in public places from Via D'Azeglio to today's Piazza Galvani. Meanwhile, the neighborhood's horses and pigs, and probably a dog or two, drank their fill of water at the nearby *guazzatoio* (watering trough).

As I walk along Via Farini, known as Via dei Libri (of books) because the book trade of the ancient university evolved here, my mind slips back to thirteenth century Bologna. The modern store windows become mirrors of the past. I look deeply into the dark inside of small *botteghe* (shops) where I see piles of manuscripts and hear spirited conversations between university rectors and the *stazionari*, who sell the books. The book industry that grew up around the ancient University of Bologna illustrates the profound influence of the institution on the city's economic history.

Students could either borrow or buy the official texts for their classes from the booksellers, whose work was considered so important that they were required to take a yearly oath in order to sell, buy, and loan books. In addition, the *stazionari* were expected to produce *pecie* (small booklets of four sheets of skins/paper, a total of sixteen pages) for all the students. The *pecie* provided excerpts of the official texts, making it much easier for the students to assimilate the material. The students usually borrowed the booklets because they were so expensive and paid fines for damage or loss. Their acquisition took place in the presence of a notary and a contract of sale was drawn up because they were easy to steal. The *notai* (notaries) had plenty of work after completing their studies at the famous university.

Shops of those dealing with the production of books—copyists, bookbinders, and miniaturists—grew up near the *stazionari*. Medieval Bologna's *cartolari* (paper makers) and *pergamenari* (parchment makers) worked hard to satisfy the needs of the university community.

I imagine the artisans busy until sunset, when the lack of light forced them to close down for the day. I see a young woman and her husband, both miniaturists, discussing a project with an important member of the Drapers' Corporation. Many women participated in the book trade as artisans. In another shop, a seated woman is copying a book from Firenze, as her husband hovers close by. Occasionally he stands at the entrance and exchanges words with passersby. A couple of doors away another woman stares at a huge Bible on the table in front of her, no doubt mulling over the task of copying it for a certain Carmelite monk who had stopped by earlier.

Under today's modern porticoes that edge the grand palazzi on Via Farini, I also glance into the store windows and enjoy window shopping in modern Bologna. Sometimes, as if by elfin magic, a black and white world of skirts, blouses, sweaters, and shoes is transformed overnight into one of soft yellow-green, vibrant orange, and rich chestnut brown as the season changes. Then I have no choice but to pause for a moment and admire.

Bologna Reflections

The Canale di Savena ran along Via Castiglione toward Piazza della Mercanzia. At its intersection with Via Farini, the Ponte di Ferro, the iron bridge, once crossed it. Via Castiglione's gentle curve makes it easy to imagine the canal flowing north, toward the flour mills, and the wooden boats with upturned ends ducking under the numerous bridges that crossed the Canale di Savena along the way.

The heavy, iron, serpent-like hooks and rings about five feet up from the pavement on the street-side flank of the Palazzo Pepoli (Via Castiglione 4–8) baffled me at first. Legend says that the hooks and rings anchored the boats that navigated the waterway that traveled toward today's Piazza di Porta Ravegnana. Via Castiglione was then the dimora of the Pepoli family, Romeo and his son Taddeo. They were rich bankers who, in the early 1300s, controlled Bologna.

The fortress-like palazzo of the Pepoli family eventually took up the entire block between Via Sampieri and Via dei Pepoli (4–10). The gothic Palazzetto Pepoli (4), built under Romeo and attributed to Antonio di Vincenzo, is the oldest construction (1300s). The giant portone opens into a cavernous space where footsteps resonate off of the immense stonewalls. Taddeo Pepoli began his neighboring fortress in 1345. The original door still remains, with its sculpted terracotta frame, while the black and white chessboard squares that line the inner border remember the family crest.

The General Council of the people gave unconditional power to Taddeo Pepoli in 1337, naming him "Protector of the Peace and of Justice" in Bologna. He constituted the first real *signoria* (a governing body) in the city's history, a direct threat to the hegemony of the Roman Catholic Church. He had to deal immediately with two interdicts placed over the city and the university by Pope Benedict XII. The interdicts threatened its economic and diplomatic situation. With some able negotiation, Taddeo Pepoli became, instead, Captain

182

of the People and Vicar of the Church in Bologna. His reign was marked by peace between factions in the city and notable diplomatic achievements in northern Italy. He died of the plague in 1347, not rousted from power by belligerent enemies.

Now, however, the usual din of passing buses, cars, and motorini makes it difficult to lose myself in the world of waterways and fourteenth century politics. Sometimes in the quiet of an early Sunday morning walk though, if I stop to close my eyes and listen, I will hear the slapping water and the dipping oars of the boats and remember "once upon a time" in Bologna.

Bologna Reflections

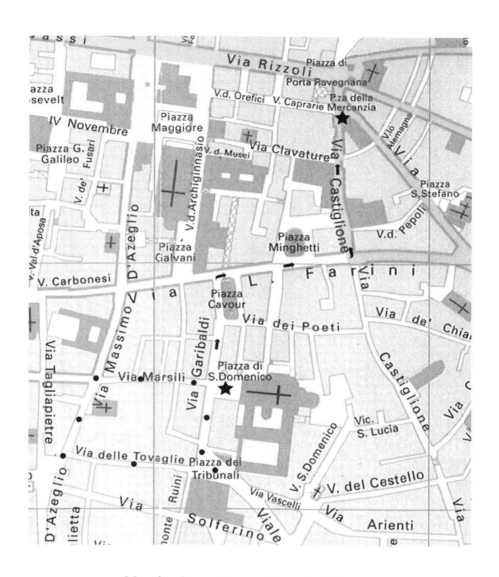

Map for *Once Upon a Time in Bologna*

Figure 29. Porta Nova

Students, Students, Everywhere

As I meander in the tiny vias—Fusari, Gargiolari, and Mareschalchi—in the neighborhood behind Piazza Maggiore called the Piccolo Quadrilatero (Little Quadrilatero), I recall daily life as it might have been in the Middle Ages. This rectangle of streets, bounded by Via Mareschalchi, Via D'Azeglio, Via IV Novembre, and Via de' Gargiolari, has been built and rebuilt over the centuries with many of the lanes and shops lost. I wander the ones that remain, imagining that time long ago when their names derived from the artisans and harried university students rushed to and from their lodgings.

The street designations suggest lively activity with the noise and congestion of a busy, productive district. A family of weavers and artisans who made *fusi* (spindles) for looms gave Via de' Fusari its name. The *mareschalchi* made horseshoes and were veterinarians for horses. The *gargiolari* worked raw hemp. On Via Battibecco, which refers to the sound of peck, peck, pecking beaks, the noise of caged chickens filled the air. Carpenters made *banzole* (cages) on Via delle Banzole. Vicolo Arolari was named for artisans who made and sold *role* (copper cake pans).

During its earliest history, when the university thrived in medieval Bologna, it was the meeting place of students and professors, artists and musicians. In fact, the schools of the Liberal Arts, including medicine, astrology, music, poetry, and grammar held lessons in various sites in the zone between Via D'Azeglio, the church of San Salvatore, and the church of San Francesco, especially near Via Portanova. The study of medicine was considered an art, like alchemy and magic, not science, and the medical student wild, to match his daring choice of studies.

Via IV Novembre has always been a passageway between Piazza Maggiore and Piazza Malpighi. It was once called Via delle Asse because of a little chapel made of wooden planks (*asse*) that leaned against the walls of Palazzo Comunale. During the Middle Ages this area was heavily populated by students, and I imagine them leaving their rented rooms in the morning to make their way to the churches, piazzas, and houses where professors waited to begin the day's lessons. Now friends meet by chance, their busy lives intersecting for a moment in the comfortable courtyard with benches and quiet.

I picture the medieval university students, their dark flowing robes pinned closed at the top, their heads capped with soft, black berets. Secondhand shops and artisan's studios also buzzed with activity then, swarming with students and professors. I watch them merge into the brown, no-nonsense world of the artisans and merchants who lived and worked in their midst, in the hectic working class quarter. Today it is mostly quiet, with the occasional pedestrian passing through.

Currently a group of artists working at the Studio d'Iconografia di Giancarlo Pellegrini, in what used to be the church of Santa Maria Labarum Coeli (Via de' Fusari 12), create Byzantine icons. In the hushed silence and shadows, I watch the artists hovering intently over their work, using only the characteristic wood, paints, and iconography of the past. Stern, flat Madonnas and saints look out with dark, haunting eyes while the Christ Child holds up his hand in blessing. Their thrones and niches are lavishly stained with gold leaf.

The Osteria del Cappello Rosso once stood at the site of today's elegant Albergo Cappello Rosso (Via de' Fusari 9). The name *"cappello rosso"* refers to the red hat that Jewish men were forced to wear as a public label of identification. In 1593 Bologna's Jewish citizens were evicted by papal edict. For centuries Jews traveling through Bologna on business, or for any other reason, could remain no more than three days. They were allowed to lodge and take their meals only in that one osteria.

The Galleria Borsellino-Falcone opposite the Questura (police headquarters) in Piazza Galileo, a modern gallery of shops, is a pleasant place to relax. Its bright openness contrasts with the narrow alleys that circumscribe it. Curved slices of white marble arches stand out against the red ocher stucco walls. Ancient white columns stand next to modern white steel supports. I stop to say hello to Paolo, a friend by chance and good fortune. After contemplating the shoes that have just arrived in his Fornasiero Calzature, I decide to get a *caffè* in a tranquil nearby bar, and then head out to consider the neighborhood's past.

The Alma Mater Studiorum is remembered in a plaque at the church of San Salvatore (Via Volto Santo 1):

> The tract of this street that goes from Piazza Maggiore to the front of this church, called in the ancient past "of Porta Nova" was, in the thirteenth, fourteenth and fifteenth centuries, the center of the Schools of Medicine, of Philosophy, of Rhetoric, of Astronomy and of the other Arts, located then in this part of the city.

I join today's midday crowd as it heads toward Piazza Malpighi on Via Portanova, approaching the Torresotto di Porta Nova. I picture myself at this same place in the year 1236. The gate ahead, one of the four still extant, opens up the Cerchia del Mille, Bologna's second ring of protective walls. As I approach the *torresotto*, I imagine clip-clopping horses, squeaking carts, and clamoring voices. Bolognesi and foreigners alike crowd me on the narrow street. Some command carts loaded with vegetables, earthenware jugs, giant pigs, or straw. Others arrive and depart on horseback. Some walk, burdened with satchels and packs on stooped shoulders. Occasionally a neighborhood church bell marks the hour, initiating its conversation with the other bells that crowd the medieval city.

In 1236 the Via delle Asse of my imagination is dank and dark near the city wall. The basilica of San Francesco d'Assisi will soon be built close to the sweetly rolling hills just outside the city wall. The chirping of the birds that flit in and out of crevices they have turned into homes and the cadence of farmers' voices on the other side remind me of the world outside the city. Bologna is expanding to accommodate the burgeoning population. The Franciscans, like the Dominicans, Benedictines, and other orders of monks that arrive in the city, are part of the force propelling it outward into the surrounding hills and fields. The presence of the Franciscans here is reassuring to the people who are building anew on top of Roman Bononia, destroyed by the Lombards in the sixth century.

I try to picture Piazza Malpighi when the monks began building their church. It's not easy, with today's rumble and thrust of the big orange city buses that launch one after the other, the zoom of the motorini, and the impatient, gear shifting push and pull of scrambling automobiles. Instead of seeing the contemporary jumble of traffic noise, the hustle and bustle of a modern city, I imagine the marketplace that once flourished in the piazza. Peddlers sell their wood, and I find pleasure in a spectacle unfolding on the piazza stage. Meanwhile, the early Franciscans lay the foundation of their majestic monument, for which the city has granted them the strip of land known as the Annunziata di Porta Stiera. They will finish the bulk of the work by 1263.

If I look beyond Piazza Malpighi from my position under Porta Nova to the apse of the Gothic church, its two slender bell towers seem to tilt ever so slightly toward each other, as if whispering, high above the modern confusion, about the life that once happened here. Perhaps they would recount the legend of the fifteenth century witch Gentile Cimieri who was supposed to have lived upstairs in the *torresotto*. I imagine her face peering out of the tower's bottom window, black hair wildly flying out in every direction, hypnotic glare pulling at us. Over her shoulder I see Lucifer's smoldering eyes and hear his relentless bellowing above the thunder and roar of the boiling inferno.

According to the chronicles of Giovanni II Bentivoglio, she was the most powerful witch ever to practice her arts in Bologna. The church tribunal at San Domenico found her guilty of witchcraft and burned her alive at the stake in Piazza Maggiore in 1498. While I am no longer sure that all those executed for witchcraft really practiced the black arts, in the mustiness and shadows of the narrow street one can call up the fearful images that superstition encourages.

I cross Piazza Malpighi, known in the Middle Ages as the Selciata di San Francesco because of the river stones that paved it, and skirt the tombs of *glossatori* Accursio and his son Francesco (1250), Odofredo (1265), and Rolandino de' Romanzi (1285). The striking memorial arks, their green-tiled roofs protecting the sepulchers underneath, celebrate the scribes who explained Justinian's code of law to the students who came to the early university. Many important professors and scholars are buried in the church and in its cloister, called the Corte dei Morti.

The basilica, primarily Gothic in style, was the first significant edifice to be built outside the Cerchia del Mille. At the time its orientation was unusual, with the facade facing the simple working class streets outside the wall instead of toward the city center.

191

Bologna Reflections

The portico of the former convent of San Francesco to the left of the church was once considered one of the most beautiful in Bologna. The lunettes of its arches depict episodes in the life of the Franciscan Sant'Antonio di Padova completed by various artists of the seventeenth century.

The architect of the basilica of San Francesco d'Assisi is anonymous. He could have been a friar just returned from France, because the use of flying buttresses and the presence of an apse with radiating chapels were new ideas originating in the French Gothic style. Antonio di Vincenzo, the architect of the church of San Petronio, became involved in about 1390. He designed the taller bell tower and the sacristy.

I enter the basilica from Piazza San Francesco, whose small, tranquil garden offers gentle green in the midst of concrete and stone. Inside, the light and air of the internal architecture direct my eyes up, up, up. Accustomed to Bologna's many Romanesque and Baroque churches, which project solidity and heaviness, I can imagine soaring upwards to heaven on the clear, piercing note of a singing hand bell. Wood panels and benches lend warmth to the immense temple. Giant pillars like colossal rust-red flowers burst open to the ceiling soaring directly to the sky. The altarpiece by the Venetians Jacobello and Pier Paolo Dalle Masegne (1388–93) is a *capolavoro* of Gothic sculpture. Its intricate, delicate white form seems almost too fragile to have withstood the centuries. The snow-white marble steeples, the abundant saints in narrow niches, and the delicately wrought designs give an overall impression of lace. Live palm trees in pots cast shadows on the walls.

I leave silence and the holy smells of wax and incense behind as I exit into the neighborhood. Via del Pratello is quiet and unpretentious. The word *"pratello"* is a diminutive for the Italian noun *"prato,"* which means an uncultivated field, one a little wild in its disorder. Perhaps grasses swayed in the breezes and in the spring red and yellow wild flowers sprouted up freely here.

The mustard gold and dirty yellow, the brown-stained peach and clay-toned stucco of the low, modest dwellings that line both sides of narrow via are flanked by equally low, narrow porticoes. Ancient, bulging, wooden beams support the first floor. Chunky, plain rectangular pillars hold the porticoes up. The working class quarter is old, albeit recently subjected to a Bolognese version of gentrification, without the fancy, elegant palazzi of Strada Maggiore and Via Galliera.

However, it is rich in simple examples of devotion. At Via del Pratello 3/A a plaque framed in terracotta depicts San Francesco of Paola, the ascetic saint from Calabria. In the fifteenth century he attended kings and emperors while he lived the Minim's life of poverty and asceticism, which was even stricter than that of the Franciscans. He looks up to heaven, of course, and his white beard reflects his old age at death (1416–1507). I search under lunettes and in corners for the numerous little shrines to Christ, the Madonna, and other saints.

Across the street, a flower box overflows with cascading red blossoms, the window's gaping green shutters open to the pleasant warm air and sunlight. Small, intimate stores and tranquil bars dot the way. Pedestrians amble with calm. A smart Bolognese signora returns home to fix the day's *pranzo*, her shopping bags, balanced on both sides, move rhythmically up and down, up and down, in sync with the up and down of her brisk stride. I pass when she stops momentarily to greet a friend who sticks her head out of a corner bar.

In the evening and late into the night the osterie and pubs of the little via welcome young and old alike. In particular, university students from all over Italy flock here. The crowds and music regularly overflow onto the sidewalk under the porticoes. Each establishment offers good food and drink, along with friendly camaraderie. A frequent destination is the Europa Cinema, a *cineclub*

Bologna Reflections

(film club) in Via Pietralata (55), which presents classic films to members and the public and often hosts cinematic events drawing large crowds.

The noise of cars and buses recedes as I continue to head away from the city on the little street that could have once been a field decorated with wildflowers. Voices travel on the breeze and occasionally the staccato click of footsteps echoes nearby. Sometimes just silence keeps me company.

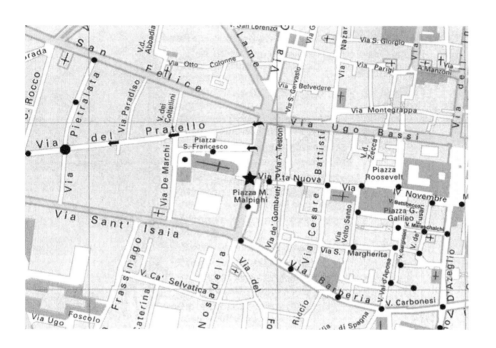

Map for *Students, Students, Everywhere*

Figure 30. Casa Grassi, Via Marsala 12

Magic in Memories

Bologna When It Rains

It rained today. Finally. Not much, but enough.
Enough to conjure up the earthy, wet smell
And the heavy, deep memories—under the porticos,
The rain crashing down. Crowds hurrying along
Not bothered much, maybe not noticing how
Comfortable a walk in Bologna is, even when it rains.

Outside, walking, without the burdensome umbrella
(That I always leave somewhere anyway).

Cars splash along in the narrow streets
Bicycles and motos catch the waves that
Fly high. I instead walk along nicely dry.

Hearing the plat, plat, plat on the red tile roofs,
Big drops, hitting the gray stone and terracotta
Hard. The blasting wind that catches unlatched
Shutters and bangs, bangs, bangs them
Against the patient palazzo wall.

I've been waiting and waiting.
Finally the clear blue sky is gone
And the gray moving sky on the march
Somewhere is flashing by, rumbling on
A roll, leaving behind floating white
Clouds that open up and then
The sunlight slices through.

Bologna when it rains—finally.

The Lesson

At nine o'clock one morning I hurried toward the Mercato Coperto, the market on Via Clavature. I was on a mission: learn how to buy fruit and vegetables as a Bolognese. I had been having trouble getting the quality produce I saw everywhere. The market was not crowded yet, but foot traffic was picking up. I went first to the little counter of a nice couple who always recognized me. They had squeezed everything that one would find in an Italian *alimentari* (grocery store) into their tiny stall. Inside, outside, the back wall, every space was covered with their wares. If I did not see what I was looking for—toilet paper, paper towel, laundry detergent, coffee pot—I just asked because they usually had it someplace in the back. They were pleasant people and always worked with me on my Italian as I struggled for the correct word.

"Buon giorno, signora," the woman greeted me as soon as I stepped up to the counter. Her husband emerged from back behind. They looked out at me and smiled. "How are you?" she continued as I took out a little scrap of white notepaper with my list written in Italian.

"Buon giorno," I returned with a smile. "I'm fine, grazie," I added, and then I began listing the things I needed. "Two bottles of mineral water, naturale, per favore, and a package of Lavazza coffee, the gold one, if you have it," I ventured.

Bologna Reflections

"Certainly," the signora responded quickly as her husband set off immediately to get the water. He returned with two varieties, which he held up for me to see. I chose the San Benedetto and, in the meantime, the signora, who had crouched behind the counter, stood up with the Lavazza coffee in its shiny gold-brick packet held aloft.

"Anything else?" she asked me.

"Basta così, that's it," I answered with a smile.

While they packed up my goods and the money exchanged hands, they asked me questions about San Francisco, the weather, the Golden Gate Bridge, and cable cars. I managed to answer in simple phrases.

"Arrivederci a presto!" We exchanged goodbyes, and I turned to my next task: learning how to buy good fruit and vegetables.

By then the market was filled with customers. I wandered through, stopping occasionally to look closely and to eavesdrop on the exchanges between them and the vendors. One signora requested bananas, but added, "one ripe and three for later." Then, as she looked at the apples, she asked the gentleman waiting on her, "Which are the best ones today? I want to eat them fresh. I like sweet ones," she added.

After the merchant explained the qualities of the varieties, she settled on the ones he recommended most highly. They continued chatting as he chose a half dozen and put them in the sack. They never stopped their friendly banter. I meandered nonchalantly by the next stall. An elderly gentleman was explaining that he wanted tomatoes for a salad. On my left I heard another signora asked for four bulbs of fennel, which she wanted to cook.

"Of course," I thought. "That's what I have to do! I can't just ask for four bananas. I have to be specific, and then they will give me what I want."

200

I decided to try. I wanted tomatoes for bruschetta so I went up to the kiosk where the elderly gentleman was paying for his order. I glanced over the tomatoes and noted the varieties, realizing how confusing it was with all the possibilities. When the vendor asked me what I would like, I uttered "Four tomatoes to make bruschetta, per favore."

Well, like magic he began to detail the qualities of longish ones with slightly green splotches emerging through the pale red skin. To my American eye, they were green and therefore unripe. I would have gone for the reddest and plumpest ones. But I nodded yes, taking his word for it. He picked out four, weighed them, and put them in a little brown sack. Meanwhile, he continued the conversation, telling me how good my Italian was and asking where I was from. We went back and forth like that and then he said, "But you will need basilico, too, right?"

When I responded "Sì," he quickly added, "I have some that is very fresh. Do you want it then?"

I signaled yes, and he found a small bunch and added it to the bag.

"What is your recipe?" he asked, and I understood him, to my amazement. So I explained as best I could, that my recipe was very simple. Just the tomatoes, chopped up, with salt and pepper and lots of good olive oil, and of course, pieces of torn up fresh basil. He shook his head approvingly, and then came the inevitable, "E poi (What else do you want)?"

I requested, "Un *finocchio* (fennel) to eat raw."

He turned toward the pile of fennel and looked through to find a chubby one and held it up for me to see. I said, "Sì, perfect" with a smile. He weighed it and wanted to know what else. I was doing so well that I decided to also get some zucchini squash and keep the exchange going. I thought quickly about how I was going to use them and decided to ask for thin, small ones if possible. I did and he immediately said, "Then you are not going to stuff them, is that right?" When I agreed, he picked out four perfect ones, weighed them, and put them in a bag.

Then he asked me if I had ever made sautéed zucchini blossoms. I answered, "No, but one day I will try it." He gave me his recipe for the dish. I listened intently but lost him as he explained in sublime detail how to make a dish that he obviously relished. I bobbed my head affirmatively, realizing I must look that one up before trying it. He didn't seem to notice that I had lost him somewhere in the middle of his explanation.

By then he had totaled the bill; I paid and, as he gave me my change and the bag of produce he smiled as pleased as I was. He welcomed me back soon and he said, "Buona giornata, signora," as I responded and walked away content, my cultural lesson of the day learned.

The Lesson

Figure 31. Under Porta Nova, Bell Towers of San Francesco

International Trade

We finished the meal with slices of still warm apple pie. "How good it is," they remarked, scraping the plates to get every smudge of juice. Then, as is required in any meaningful international trade agreement, Clara and I promised to exchange written recipes. It was a special family meal on All Saints Day, not only an Italian national holiday and Roman Catholic holy day, but also Clara's birthday. Tortellini in Brodo had been her contribution to the meal, the American Apple Pie mine. The family was hers, but that day our exchange pulled me close to them, as if I were a welcome American cousin come to visit.

But that's getting ahead of the story.

I set out for Clara's at nine that morning, meandering toward the historic center on little side streets from Via Broccaindosso to Via San Mamolo. There was no traffic so early on a holiday. Even grand Strada Maggiore, usually congested with buses, cars and motorini, was silent. Cold, damp fog hung heavily over the world around me. I could hear only my footsteps but, surprisingly, did not feel lonely. I felt privy to the secrets of another time, another world, imagining myself on that ancient Roman road, the Via Emilia, or as a visitor to the dark, narrow streets of the medieval city. Looking back on that day, I guess this story began there, when the writer lost herself in the place and the moment, her memories traversing the city's ancient past and present, bumping into friendship and warmth on a cold day.

Clara was waiting for me outside the door to her flat, arms open to embrace me. She takes life seriously, her large dark eyes reflecting her sincere nature and her quest to understand everything about the world around her. I have sometimes seen her eyes smile softly when she notices a fragile wildflower nudging up through the rocks along the mountain path or when she engages in conversation with a young child we meet on one of our many excursions. She welcomed me that day with anticipation for our culinary collaboration.

"Benvenuta, Mary, how are you?" she asked.

"Bene," I responded, as our cheeks touched in the traditional both-sides double *bacio*. We entered the flat, and the wonderful aroma of simmering broth already drifting in from the kitchen, steaming up the windows. "This is certainly different than ordering the tortellini dish in a restaurant and waiting at the table for it to arrive!" I thought, imagining a wide bowl filled with hot, savory broth, floating puffs of tortellini mantled in wisps of freshly grated Parmigiano Reggiano cheese.

Clara and her husband Renato were already preparing the filling. He had just returned from his morning walk to and from Piazza Maggiore, with cheeks still rosy from the cold November air. "I'm surprised we didn't we meet each other on the way," he said, "I just came in myself." As Renato put the mortadella through the meat grinder, Clara went to check the slices of pork loin sautéing in a small pan on a low gas flame. Renato is as tall and quiet mannered as Clara is short and very outgoing. Sort of like Tom and I, except that my husband is the social one.

"What is your family recipe for the broth?" I asked Clara while I stood watching her turn the meat. I had spent enough time in Bologna to know that every family has its own time-honored recipe for meat broth.

"Our recipe requires different cuts and kinds of meat," she explained, "Some bones and vegetables—a carrot or two, celery, onion, and a garlic clove." She had used a beef bone, a bit of chicken, some beef tenderloin, and brisket of pork. Initially about four inches of water had covered the meat and vegetable combination in the stewing pot, which needed to simmer for a total of at least two hours.

Then Renato added, "You know Mary, the best broth is that made with capon." I was surprised. "Is the flavor rich enough?" I questioned. "Assolutamente," they answered in chorus. And Clara assured me "In the winter months we always use a plump capon."

We turned our attention back to the filling for the tortellini. Each family also has its own version. The basic ingredients are more or less the same but the amounts and the specifics vary considerably. To genuine Bolognese mortadella, fresh pork loin, and aged Parmigiano Reggiano cheese, some add chicken or turkey breast, beef, or veal. Some families use butter and others olive oil to brown the pork and chicken before grinding them. Some use the meat and poultry raw. Most of the recipes call for prosciutto di Parma, although Clara's does not. The spices vary, but each recipe usually includes freshly ground nutmeg.

When the pork slices were ready to add to the filling, Clara motioned to the table where the ingredients for the pasta dough awaited. "Now we begin the most important task," she said happily.

Bologna Reflections

I was impressed that she had enough confidence to wait until the day of the pranzo to make it. "I think I would have started yesterday," I told her, laughing, "in case the batch didn't turn out well."

"But Mary," she reminded me, "you must remember that I have been making tortellini my whole life." From the time she could barely reach the tabletop she had made them with her grandmother and mother, with her siblings and cousins, aunts, friends, and then with her own children. She had no reason to worry.

Clara's huge, well-worn, wooden pastry board occupied at least half of the tabletop, which itself almost filled the small kitchen. A soft mound of about two cups of white flour sat in the center. Just a bit of semolina had been added, giving it a delicate yellow cast. Clara scooped out the center of the mound, making a well clear down to the board, big enough for the four large eggs that she cracked open. Next she beat the eggs with a fork, keeping them in the center of the flour without taking any in. After she had done that for a minute or so, she began to gather some of the flour into the burgeoning well as she continued to beat the eggs in a steady swirling rhythm, the fork striking the board underneath to keep time. With expert gestures she kept the walls of the flour from caving in. She made it look so easy, but I had already tried this at home and knew it took true skill to keep the eggs from overflowing their flour bounds and flooding the flat board, the table, and the floor. Clara could even talk while she worked and not lose a drop of the liquid. I watched her every movement intently, hoping to understand her skill.

Soon the mixture was dense enough for her to manage with her hands. It was time to knead the dough. "We must scrape the board to remove any hard bits and excess flour," she explained. I cleaned the area well with a spatula and then watched as she began to push the mass with the heel of the right hand, while stretching it back with the left. She folded the stretched piece over, turned

208

the whole mass clockwise, and started over again. She would continue that way for as long as it took to transform the blend of lumpy egg and flour into a warm satiny, golden puff of living pasta dough.

I could see and feel it happening when she allowed me to spell her. "The kneading time can vary," she clarified, "according to the day's weather and humidity, the flour, the eggs ..." I had often worked with pastry and bread dough and therefore anticipated the tactile marvel when, at a precise moment, the ingredients would marry and become something else altogether.

"There," Clara said, "We are finished." We had worked the dough for about twenty minutes.

I breathed in the aroma of egg-laced flour, rich, full, and oh-so-familiar. I could see the scene as if from outside the room: the three friends around the table, the exchange of recipes and friendship. Even the language difficulties were evaporating, the words coming more easily, at times not even necessary.

We covered the dough in plastic wrap to keep it from drying out. It would "rest" for an hour before the flattening and stretching process could begin. We scraped and cleaned the board again so that we could turn our attention to the apple pie.

Renato was paging through the newspaper, half reading and half listening to Clara and me as we searched for the appropriate pie pans. I explained that a round shape worked best, one with a short lip on the sides. After rummaging around in the cupboard for a couple of minutes, we found two pans with possibilities.

We started peeling the apples, which had come from their trees in Gabba, a tiny mountain village to the south of Bologna. They were misshapen and wormy, but crisp and tasty. We would need at least ten apples per pan, because hers were on the small side. She only had fifteen so the extras I had brought would come in handy.

We sat at the table and talked, working methodically, one apple at a time. Clara was excited with anticipation as I had been while learning to make the pasta dough. We talked about Luisa, her cousin and my friend, while the long rings of apple peels dropped into the bowls on our laps and we halved, quartered, cored, and sliced each one. Clara talked with nostalgia of Luisa's many visits to Bologna and the mountains south of the city. We talked about how wonderful it would be for Clara to visit her elderly cousin in California. She had never been to the United States and had always hoped to visit the family there. We talked about our children and families and about our international exchange in the kitchen. Finally the big pot was sufficiently full of apples, even though we had managed a nibble or two as we worked. We tossed the slices in lemon juice and put them aside.

When the pasta dough had rested long enough, Clara called Renato, who was the expert on the pasta machine, and he joined us at the table. He took small portions of pasta and stretched them through the machine, one deft hand working the lever, the other catching the stretched length as it emerged from underneath. He put each piece of dough through the roller twice, folding it for a second time through, lightly flouring the roller to keep the dough from sticking as it was pressed through progressively tighter settings. The strips of fresh pasta became thinner, silkier, and more manageable.

"We can stop now," Renato explained, "I think that the filling will be just barely visible through the stretched pasta dough, the final test!" He laid the first strip on the board and Clara cut it into inch and a half squares. We dotted each square with a marble-sized portion of the filling. Each square was then folded in half diagonally, to about one eighth inch from the opposite edge, to form a triangle.

210

I enjoyed listening to the back and forth banter as they teased each other about the characteristics of one another's finished product. The trickiest maneuver came next. The two points of the folded edge had to be brought together to form a thumb-sized circle, and gently pressed, definitely a case of "easier said than done."

The three of us worked over the huge wooden board. We fell into a rhythm, or at least they did. My personal rhythm was very slow, each of my tortellini a work of art or at least work. They not only managed to fly through the process of folding and pinching but also to watch what I was doing and give me tips along the way. When we arrived at the last portion of dough to squeeze through the pasta machine, Clara and I moved back to "Project American Apple Pie."

Before beginning the pastry dough, we dressed the apples, adding a dash of salt, sugar, a little flour, cinnamon, and nutmeg. I mentioned that my father loved what he called French Apple Pie, which contains raisins as well. Renato said he liked raisins, too, so we put some in a little hot water to plump them for a few minutes. One of the pies would be French Apple.

Meanwhile, I measured the flour into the bowl and mixed in the salt with a fork. Adding chunks of cold butter a portion at a time, I gripped two knives, one in each hand, and they clicked as I crossed them, cutting the butter into the flour mixture. When it had become pale yellow and pebbly, I added the blend of water and lemon juice I'd prepared in advance. The moment had arrived when those ingredients also united into a soft, not too sticky, not too dry manageable mass of dough. It was time to roll out the piecrust.

Clara turned the oven on to heat while we worked the pastry to fit the two baking pans. "Now I have two more examples of pie plates to add to my catalog of experiences," I laughed. Pie plates are not readily available in Italy.

Bologna Reflections

She drained the now-plump raisins while I rolled out the first bottom crust. We decided that Renato's pie would be rectangular with raisins. The part that she and Renato had been waiting for was when I crimped the edges to make the confection look like the pie sitting on the windowsill in the Donald Duck comics. Clara took over the task with enthusiasm at one point and exclaimed when she finished, "I always wanted to know how to do that part," her eyes sparkling.

The pies in the oven, we turned our attention to cleaning up again and, when that was done, set the table. The broth was heating and the tortellini sat in a single layer on two white dishtowels. Now the fragrance of the bubbling apple pie in the oven filled the kitchen, too, and floated out into the living room where Renato was watching the midday news program on television. All was well.

The doorbell rang just as we finished the table. It was Paola, their daughter. "Happy birthday, Mom," she murmured as soon as she embraced Clara. "How nice it will be to celebrate together, Mary" she added, as she greeted me as well.

Then Clara carefully dropped the four portions of tortellini into the simmering broth. A little glass bowl of grated Parmigiano awaited us on the table, along with water and wine. The other dishes that would follow the *primo piatto* (first course) sat to the side.

Clara announced, "The tortellini are ready. Tutti a tavola!" She served each of us an ample portion, and the aromatic steam curled up under our noses as we waited for her to join us. We passed the Parmigiano Reggiano around while Renato poured the frizzy red wine, which is produced by the family. "Tanti auguri," we all chimed together, as we raised our glasses to salute Clara on her birthday.

Then the fun began. The teasing that went along with eating tortellini that the family had just made together was part of the tradition. The shapes were commented upon, positive and negative aspects noted without mercy. Laughing all around. The comments began regarding mine. Even I could distinguish them. Each held together well because the points where I had pinched the ends were too hard. No one complained so much that they wouldn't eat it, but I had learned my lesson: a delicate hand is more satisfactory when it comes to pinching pasta.

The next course centered on the *bollita*, or meat that had cooked in the simmering broth. *Salsa verde* (pesto with a base of parsley), enhanced each bite. As accompaniments we enjoyed a variety of vegetables marinated in vinegar: mushrooms, eggplant, artichokes, and tender little onions. The typical Bolognese bread, white with a dry yet soft texture and crisp, thick, cracker-like crust attended the course.

Clara opened Paola's small gifts. The blue pen and elegant sheets of writing paper brought a pleased smile to her face. Then we all smiled contentedly as dessert was served: warm American Apple Pie with Gelato alla Crema. "Happy birthday, Clara!" we exclaimed.

After many years, our ongoing collaboration still brings us pleasure, as do the memories of that day when Clara's family became mine.

Figure 32. Salumeria in the Quadrilatero

Baloney—Bologna

"Baloney!" When my dad says "baloney" he means "Nonsense, whatever you're saying is pure nonsense." The word seems perfectly suited to the lunchmeat I ate as a child. Baloney. Nonsense, pure indeterminate nonsense inside two slices of white poufy Wonder Bread, a little mayo—lunch. Baloney has always been on my "no thank you" list.

I have to admit that part of my suspicion of the American sandwich meat came from the spelling on the package "b-o-l-o-g-n-a" and the pronunciation "ba-low-nee" that never quite jived for me. "Where in the world did this come from?" I used to wonder.

Now I know. What a coincidence that one of my favorite places in the world is a city named Bologna, correctly pronounced "bo-low-nya," and in whose honor my country has named a luncheon meat. Everything makes sense now, in an American kind of way. We pronounce it American style, of course, and our luncheon meat is nothing like the renowned Mortadella Bolognese, its inspiration.

I did not taste it on my first visit to the city in 1994. I could not bring myself to eat a sausage that resembled baloney but had, in addition, chunks of fat scattered throughout. "No, no thank you," I would say, "I'll take some of the Genoa salami instead." Eventually though, an occasion presented itself that

215

Bologna Reflections

required me to partake. Perhaps I found myself at a reception, a long table spread with delicacies and someone saying, "You must try this mortadella, it is truly Mortadella Bolognese at its very best." And so I did.

American baloney is tan, firm, and tastes like nothing in particular. Mortadella Bolognese is creamy pink, subtly spiced, and melts in my mouth. Since ancient times Bologna has been renowned for her pork products. Even the Roman Emperor Augustus sought the sausages of Bononia. It is believed that a stone slab, with a mortar and pestle carved in relief, conserved today in the Museo Civico Archeologico in Bologna, commemorates the Roman city's famous sausage. Those simple instruments were once necessary for its preparation because the pork was pounded into a creamy puree.

It is also thought that the Galli Boi, Celtic tribes that descended on Bologna in about 300 BC, introduced the raising of swine and the art of making salami to the city, whose surrounding farmlands offered the perfect environment. Ever since the Middle Ages Bologna has been famous beyond its borders for the mortadella that is sometimes known simply as Bologna.

The genuine mortadella must be made with sixty percent pure lean pork of the highest grade, either loin, shank, or shoulder; forty percent fat from the cheek of the pig; a natural casing; salt; whole black peppercorns; and a mix of spices, none of which dominate. They could be cinnamon, cloves, nutmeg, mace, coriander, star anise, and cumin. No chemical preservatives are allowed, and neither garlic nor pistachios would be found in an authentic Bolognese recipe. One way to judge a slice of mortadella is to notice whether or not the meat and the squares of fat separate when served. They should not.

Today the meat is cleaned and passed through the grinder multiple times until a very fine texture is achieved. The cubes of velvety fat are slowly stirred into the creamy paste, along with the spices. The mixture is then stuffed into the casing, which can be of different sizes. The plump, squat, egg-shaped sausages are cured in a cool area for a short time and then roasted slowly, for up to twenty hours, hanging on rotating racks in specially designed ovens called *stufe*. The temperature is closely regulated by the *stufini*, specialists in the art of cooking the mortadella.

I often walk in the Quadrilatero and gawk at the storefront windows of any number of delicatessens. The abundance of delicacies mesmerizes me and certainly stimulates my appetite. The mortadella sausages hang there. Together they preside over the giant wheels of pale, golden Parmigiano Reggiano that sit regally under them to tempt the defenseless passersby.

Many traditional Bolognese recipes include mortadella. For the filling of tortellini Bolognesi it is ground and mixed with other ingredients. Meatballs or meatloaf would also include a certain portion. It can be served as a hot antipasto, cut into sticks, breaded, and fried. Often a cold antipasto platter will offer it, either thinly sliced or cubed, along with other cured meats, cheese, and marinated vegetables.

~

May 2002

The three of us were arranged around the room-sized dining table, which was covered with a crisp, white tablecloth. A huge platter of meats and cheese sat in the center. A two-quart green bottle of the family's red wine was next to it. Small white bowls were placed here and there, filled with black and green olives, carrots, mushrooms, and artichoke hearts marinated in olive oil. A stainless steel bowl lined with a white paper napkin held a variety of crackers and slices of Bolognese bread. The table was set for four, but the signora would never sit down to join us. She flitted around insisting that we all eat and drink.

Bologna Reflections

Signor Casanova, seventy years plus, tall and robust, sat across the table from me. His thirty-year-old daughter Emanuela listened quietly. She was smiling, happy to have arranged the encounter. I burrowed in my bag, searching for the tape recorder, and asked him if he would object to my recording our conversation. While the normally gruff ex-butcher filled our respective glasses with brother-in-law Massimo's wine, which would ease us into the interview, he assured me that no, recording our exchange would not be a problem.

I had arrived at about six p.m., the appointed time, with trepidation, not expecting an easy conversation. Signor Casanova had rarely spoken with me before, beyond the initial perfunctory greeting. He still used the formal "you" when we did exchange words, even though we had been acquainted for eight years and I had often been a guest at the family's dinner table. He would normally greet me cordially and then immediately seek refuge in his study while the rest of us would visit. He would lend me books about Bologna's past and occasionally discuss a particular historical detail, but that was about it. Our relationship had always been amicable but distant.

As soon as I arrived that day I realized that this visit would be different because Signor Casanova was animated and smiling as he met me at the door himself. Usually Emanuela or the signora would let me in. We exchanged pleasantries and he, evidently anxious to begin, rushed directly to the dining room table with me close behind. He sat down immediately, motioning me to follow his lead. He began the discourse as if he had been waiting his whole life to unburden himself of the details.

When he gave me the go-ahead, I quickly turned on the recorder. He ignored it, talking to me directly. The signora brought the platter to me again and again, holding it squarely up under my nose so I could not refuse to take another morsel. Eating was not negotiable.

We clinked our half-filled glasses around the table, sloshing the slightly frizzy red wine, as I gathered a few bits of meat and cheese onto my plate. Signor Casanova talked, hardly pausing to breathe. Emanuela and I sat back and enjoyed the moment, while her mother darted here and there serving us all. The little recorder, likewise, whirred on, trying to keep up with the spirited signori.

"Signora," Signor Casanova said to me, breathlessly, "please tell me what you want me to tell you. I guess I should have at least asked."

"That's fine," I answered, "You're doing fine, sir, please tell me about your life as a butcher in Bologna."

He had already begun to do just that, interjecting profuse commentary on details as he went. He jumped back quickly into his monologue, regardless of the commotion that steadily mounted in the room.

The interview evolved quickly into a regular family gathering and I quietly folded my notes and put them back into my bag. Obviously, I was not in control. The tape recorder spun on to capture his words and the chaos erupting around us at the table. As often happened when I visited, the rest of the family had been advised of my arrival so eventually they all stopped in to see me, including little Elsa, the Casanova's three-year-old granddaughter. The interview-in-name-only continued relentlessly. Signor Casanova refused to change course.

Lucky for me, the tape recorder kept pace with him: I could not have taken notes fast enough to capture all the details he shared. He spoke rapidly in a no-nonsense fashion and announced first that the pastas are Bologna's real gift to the culinary world, the tortellini, lasagne, and tagliatelle. Then he described the history of making *salume* in Emilia and mortadella in particular in Bologna. Signor Casanova's great-grandfather, grandfather, and father had all been butchers before him. Neither of his sons would carry on the tradition, though. One is an attorney, the other an engineer, while his daughter is a medical doctor. He retired about thirty-five years ago but not from working. He still has business interests that occupy his time.

I listened and responded to Signor Casanova, while visiting with the other family members. Occasionally I steered the discourse in a direction that interested me, namely his reflections on Bologna's past. I turned the tape over.

He explained his family history, which began in Lucca. His pleasure intensified visibly when he began to discuss Signor Ivo Galletti, the owner of Alcisa, one of today's most important producers of mortadella in Bologna. They have had a long professional relationship and have great esteem for each other. Signor Galletti has been named a Cavaliere del Lavoro for his achievements in the making of salami, a title bestowed by the Italian government. The original Alcisa establishment was near Porta San Vitale, but now it is in the nearby town of Zola Predosa. Scenes from the 1971 film *The Mortadella*, with Sofia Loren, were actually filmed in the old Alcisa salumeria in Bologna.

Signor Casanova's family once raised swine in the countryside south of Bologna, and he used to sell pigs to Signor Galletti for making the mortadella. That is how their professional relationship came about. Then he described the friendships and work relationships that developed around the buying and selling of the swine. Bologna's meat market, where he had served as a butcher, was once located near Porta Lame, on the city's northwest corner just outside the gate. However, the business deals would take place at the old Bar Centrale at the corner of Via Ugo Bassi and Via dell'Indipendenza, where McDonald's is today. Every Friday afternoon the buyers and sellers would meet there to negotiate transactions while they socialized. In fact, there was a special meeting point where the merchants and producers would congregate for each product sold in the city. For instance, the sheep would be bartered in Via Pescherie Vecchie and the grain traded where the Sala Borsa is today.

At eight p.m. I tried to end the discourse, but Signor Casanova wanted to continue talking. I had opened the floodgates, and I had no idea how to close them again. None of us did. His children and their significant others were all there by then, about seven of us in all. A half hour later his daughter, son, daughter-in-law, and I moved toward the door. We had already missed our dinner reservation. It didn't matter. We had cleaned up everything on the platter and in the bowls, good substantial Bolognese fare.

As he stood up to usher us to the door, Signor Casanova was flushed and happy. His warm and paternal manner included me in the embrace of the family gathering. My initial concern had been misplaced. The conversation with the stern *signore* did not go forward as I had planned, but luckily I had asked the correct question, "Signor Casanova, will you tell me about yourself?"

Everyone has a story to tell. He did. After that day I also had another baloney story. Somehow it had evolved though, like Cinderella had into a princess, from no-nonsense baloney into succulent Mortadella Bolognese.

Figure 33. Palazzo Monti-Salina, Via Barberia 13

Romance In Time

An evening at an old-fashioned osteria, a simple neighborhood gathering point where one goes to share a glass of wine with friends, can provide a nostalgic glance back in time. A few in Bologna still carry on the old traditions and a gathering can evoke the spirit of days gone by.

Bologna has long been noted for her osterie. Since the eleventh century students from all over the world have arrived to study at the Università di Bologna. An osteria was the perfect place to pass the evening carousing or carrying on late night, wine-fueled debates. In the thirteenth century about 150 of them hosted merchants and pilgrims traveling the important north-south routes that passed through the city. They stopped to eat a basic meal (pasta, beans, cheese, or local sausage) and drink the wine, usually made or bottled on the premises. Perhaps their most glorious moment occurred when Pope Clement V crowned Charles V Holy Roman Emperor in Bologna in 1530. Throngs of foreigners converged on the city to participate in the coronation events finding shelter, food, and company at the osterie.

The official public notice of an osteria was a leafy branch, illuminated at night by a lantern. Each enterprise would also affix a sign outside with its own symbol, an animal or other image, plus an indication of its specialty, which could have been anything from soup to eggs, cheese, meatballs, or sausage. The Osteria del Sole (Vicolo Ranocchi 1/D) once specialized in frittatas, for instance, and the symbol on its sign was and still is the sun. Open since 1465 even now it offers hospitality to all manner of guests: students and professors, fruit and vegetable vendors from the nearby market, tourists, and old-timers. Today no food is served so patrons at del Sole are encouraged to bring their own snacks to accompany the wine. Once upon a time, it was bottled in the gigantic cantina down below. Now it arrives already confectioned but chosen by the expert host with great care.

The occupation of host, characterized by a passion for the art of wine, has always been more a calling than a simple job. In the past the secrets of the trade were passed on from one generation to the next, with an initiation period that could last for years. In the 1300s the hosts united into a secret corporation and, as the centuries went forward, they kept alive the tradition and passed on its mysteries to those who followed.

The spirit of camaraderie that animates Bologna's osterie has not changed and neither has the availability of wine, always integral to the life of the city in general for families both rich and poor. The names of the city's streets hint at this. For instance, the name of Via Castellata, between Via Santo Stefano and Via Castiglione, could refer to the shape of the space made by its intersection with Via Castiglione and Via Rialto where it resembles a *castellata*, a gigantic elongated barrel that contains 211 gallons of wine. Others believe that there was once an Osteria Castellata at the intersection.

Over time the city's osterie became a place of popular culture. Tradesmen, artisans, farmers, laborers, porters, and mendicants could be found whiling the hours away. The osteria was a counterpart to the café, which usually accommodated the upper and intellectual classes, the artists, aristocrats, scholars, and writers.

Osterie have sometimes had a questionable reputation, reinforced perhaps by the fourteenth century law forbidding children, nobles, married men, and merchants from frequenting such places. Although the law was revoked a long time ago, some people continued to look down on them and their patrons.

In today's Bologna an osteria is usually an animated place to sit around a table and drink, eat, and enjoy an evening with friends. In the dimly lit and intimate world, events can even take on a dreamlike quality. They certainly did for me one time, an evening of romance and what might have been—at least that's how I remember it.

~

May 1994

One Friday evening my friend Noa and I arrived right on time at the Osteria del Moretto just outside the ancient Porta San Mamolo. We both thought that ten p.m. was already on the late side to begin a social event. Obviously, we had never been to an osteria. The place was almost empty, although we found two or three of our fellow classmates at the long table in the back. We were all attending an Italian language school for adults in Bologna, which had organized the outing at the osteria to introduce us to another facet of Bolognese culture and to allow us a chance to socialize.

Over the next two hours other students arrived and the table eventually overflowed. Massimo, the director of the school, was there as were Roberta and Stefania, two of the teachers. A group of Bolognese males, teetering on the brink of middle age, had also attached themselves to our group. Meanwhile the place settled deeper into darkness and noise and, in time, strains of lovely guitar melodies managed to reach the table from some unseen corner.

Bologna Reflections

My mood became dreamy as the red wine, bolstered by nibbles of *crostini* that had somehow materialized, smoothed the edges of the awkwardness I felt. I didn't say much. I preferred small gatherings, quiet conversations. As a middle-aged woman, I was not used to spending an evening out with friends the age of my sons. I had left them and my husband at home while I studied Italian in Bologna for two months. Most of the time I was exhilarated by the adventure of it, but that week I had been feeling particularly lonely.

Suddenly I heard a voice telling me that I spoke Italian *benissimo*. I sensed a particular man trying to break through the little wall of isolation I had unconsciously wrapped around myself. Conversation was difficult with all the noise and having to converse in Italian made it even more so. Not wishing to be rude I did my best to talk to Alessandro, the quietest of the four men who had joined our table. His calm in the confusion of the noisy osteria kept my attention and suited my mood. We chatted for a while, and when I realized that Alessandro's interest in me had potential romantic overtones, I began to pay more attention to him. He was tall and thin, with dark hair and intense brown eyes framed in wire-rimmed glasses. He seemed sincere, maybe even too serious. A neatly trimmed black beard accentuated his pensive features, although this memory could very well be an invention, something that I've added in recollecting the encounter, to make him seem more "the philosopher."

As I leaned across the table to re-explain something I had said, he blurted out, "But you're married!" He had noticed the wedding ring on my left hand for the first time.

I said, somewhat confused, "Sì—yes, very married." He turned to his friends and I went from being in the wings to center stage. The men became strangely hushed and I overheard him say "And she even said it like an Italian, her answer was Italian. I can't believe she's American—and married." His consternation surprised me. At most I had expected that a mere gentle flirtation was evolving. Then, in the din of all those tables full of loud, spirited, Friday night revelers, I lost the rest of the friends' animated exchange.

Evidently, the seeds of romantic imaginings found fertile soil in the fog that enveloped me in the legendary Osteria del Moretto that night. Meeting in an osteria can do that. It is a world outside of time that wants a story. And ours did continue, at least for a little while.

Later he excused himself with a smile and left the table. In about an hour I crawled out from my seat in the corner and gathered my coat and purse. As I walked from the back room toward the front, I heard someone calling. It was Alessandro. He was sitting at a small, crowded table near the door. I went over to say goodbye, surprised that he was still there. He reached out, took both of my hands in his, and looked up at me, as I said "Goodbye, Alessandro, I'm pleased to have met you."

He stopped me before I could continue, and said quietly, "I know that. I know because you see, I know we will be together. I'll wait for the next life. I'll wait for you." His eyes burned deeply into mine and the space between us heated up noticeably. I stood speechless for a few seconds. Finally I took my hands away from his and mumbled something about getting home. It had not been the perfunctory arrivederci I had anticipated.

To be honest, my heart yearned, just for a split second, to see where the evening could take me, us. But I left quietly. I had never expected romantic interludes while I traveled alone nor had I imagined that uninvited Romance would find me anyway.

As I walked home to my apartment on Via San Vitale, I shrugged off the encounter. But occasionally my thoughts have returned to that evening, to the quiet conversation Alessandro and I had in that noisy osteria. If I had been free, who knows what might have happened? Romance, ah sweet romance, what would life be without it? Perhaps this romantic memory still flickers precisely because reality never intruded to snuff it out.

~

June 2002

I returned to the Osteria del Moretto at my husband's insistence. We had watched a television special in which the musician Francesco Guccini discussed his experiences in the osterie of Bologna and particularly at the Osteria del Moretto. When I told him that Guccini was talking about the place where my romantic Bolognese encounter had occurred, Tom immediately picked it for our evening together. Besides having a truly romantic soul, he was curious. He knew my osteria story well.

We walked there, hand in hand, enjoying the silent streets of Bologna on a Monday evening, which happened to be a holiday. Suffocating heat had driven most Bolognesi away, to places swept by the breezes of the Adriatic Sea. Our walk was leisurely as we enjoyed being outside after sunset. We found tranquility at the Moretto as well. When we entered, the host, a tall, thin man in his forties, left a table of friends and greeted us warmly. People in groups of twos and threes sat at the small wooden tables. The atmosphere was quiet, the conversations muted and intimate. We were all in the front room where it was cooler, thanks to an overhead fan stirring the sultry air. Occasionally laughter from the host's table punctuated the calm.

Looking around I saw details I didn't remember. The huge wood bar dominated the room. Antique glass chandeliers bathed the space with soft yellow light and showed off the walls. They had been painted creamy white on top and brick red on the bottom and decorated with what seemed a random collection of paraphernalia: extravagant and colorful vintage posters, sepia-toned photographs of times past, and framed artists' sketches and paintings. Bottles stood flank to flank, lining shelves in every corner.

The young waitress approached the table, greeted us shyly, and asked what we would like. Tom ordered two glasses of prosecco and then requested that she recommend a red wine. He enjoys exploring the world of wine when we are traveling, especially local ones. He was pleased with the unpretentious place and the occasion, his blue eyes animated, his smile easy. So often he was at home working to support his wife's exploration of Bologna's hidden treasures. It was nice to be there together for a change.

The waitress hesitated. "I am very new at this job," she explained, "but I will ask Franco to help you." We saw her whisper to the man who had welcomed us earlier. He stood up quickly and came to our table.

"So, what can I do to help you?" he asked. He seemed pleased that we had asked for advice.

"Can you suggest a red wine that would go well with an antipasto and plate of assorted crostini?" Tom ventured, in his more than adequate Italian. Our host suggested a couple of red wines and we chose a Cabernet Riserva '98 from Alto Adige. In the meantime, the waitress brought us our prosecco and the antipasti we had ordered. The bruschetta were generous slices of lightly grilled bread loaded with chopped tomatoes, olive oil, and basil. Another platter held small rounds of bread spread with a variety of toppings: delicate liver pâté, a spread flavored lightly with earthy truffles, and another topped with pears, walnuts, and Brie. While we sipped the wine and sampled the snacks, we chatted with the host who answered our questions about the Osteria del Moretto's past and present.

The name was adopted in the 1970s, he said, when Mauro Rovinetti, dubbed "the Moretto," bought the locale. His nickname derives from the name of four of the face cards in the Bolognese tarot deck, spear-wielding knights with jaunty hats. Examples, of course, are displayed in the anteroom.

The buildings date to the 1400s when the Jesuits constructed a monastery and little church on the site. The monastery structure has remained almost intact. The osteria's story began in the second half of the nineteenth century. City ordinances had required the gates of the protective wall to be closed at sunset. Inns immediately outside the gate were required to provide lodging as well as food to travelers who arrived after sunset. The original osteria was located at this critical position just outside Porta San Mamolo, a main route from Tuscany.

In 1927 Delio Gandolfi assumed proprietorship of the Osteria del Voltone delle Acque (of the waters), the Moretto's predecessor, named for a well that provided drinkable fresh water then and still exists in the cantina. He and his family ran it from 1927 until 1969. Gandolfi brought his own grapes in from the countryside and, down in the cantina under the inn, made wine that he sold to *trattore* and individuals.

Wine is no longer made at the osteria but plenty of drinking, eating, and friendly gatherings keep the spirit alive. Eventually our host went back to his table of friends, and we were alone. His story of the osteria's past, along with the reminders of those times in Bologna everywhere we looked, wrapped us in nostalgia. Gradually our musings turned toward us and that quiet moment together.

"Is this romantic enough for you," I teased my husband as he reached across the table to hold my hands between his. The wine Franco had suggested was good, the subsequent plate of cheese and basket of bread simple and tasty.

"What do you think?" he answered. He was smiling broadly and lifted my hands to his lips and kissed them.

Tom has the bluest eyes, like the sea when the sky is clear and blue on a sunny day. It's easy for me to get lost in them. When he's content they sparkle and spidery smile lines etch the outer corners. He had come to meet me in Bologna. At the Osteria del Moretto my two worlds—American and Italian—were united.

"Thanks for being here with me," I said and added a question I knew he would understand. "It won't be long now. Are you going to renew?" We have a long-standing ritual of renewing our marriage commitment each year on our wedding anniversary. Our 32nd was just a few days off. "Yes," he answered, "I guess so. The next year could be a big one, so now's not the time to jump ship and miss out!"

This answer, like the question, was no surprise. One of us always answers that way. We are optimistic and satisfied when we consider our relationship. And we still really do like being together.

It was one a.m. when we bid our host and his friends goodbye. Outside the streets had grown even quieter. We walked along silently for a while, holding hands. I was thinking about Bologna's ancient times and the romantic tale that usually flits through my mind whenever I pass the Osteria del Moretto. Our footsteps echoed under the stone portico of Via D'Azeglio as we went toward the historic center. "This time the Romance was for real, sweetheart," I whispered to Tom. He squeezed my hand as we continued on our way.

Figure 34. A Walk Under the Portico

The Gift

I pushed open the heavy wooden door of a music store called Orpheus and entered into a small room overflowing with university students, racks of sheet music, ancient instruments, and shiny new ones. Guitars, violins, and even an exotic item or two, a drum from Africa and a wooden flute from South America, hung from floor to ceiling and covered every inch of wall space. The large display window had caught my attention as I wandered in the narrow, porticoed streets of Bologna's university district. My first reaction was to wait for a quieter time, but I would be leaving for home in a couple of days and I still had to buy my son the gift he had requested. Orpheus seemed the perfect place.

A gentleman approached immediately, in spite of the chaos. He was in his early forties, short, with black hair and thick, dark-rimmed glasses. His large doe-eyes smiled in welcome, as he asked in formal Italian, "Prego, signora, can I assist you?"

"Sì, signore, grazie," I responded. "I'm looking for a gift for my son, who is a musician and requested an alto recorder. I see you have a number of recorders here in the display," and I turned to the glass cabinet to my right. "But I can't distinguish an alto from a soprano!"

"Benissimo," he said, his eyes animated all at once. "It would please me to assist you. You see, the alto recorder is my specialty. I teach students from the university and I play in a small professional ensemble." Unlocking the cabinet, he continued, "Please tell me about your son. What is his name?"

"Si chiama Filippo," his name is Philip, I answered, and then described him to the professor, his musical experience and his personality: a young man of eighteen, talented, whose soul the world glimpsed when he played thin, lilting melodies on his soprano recorder, or on his flutes and pipes from around the world.

He shook his head slowly as he closed the display and earnestly explained, "Signora, these instruments will not satisfy your son's needs. I'm sorry. They are for people without serious intention or perhaps for beginners. Do you have some time you can spend here while I demonstrate my meaning?"

"Yes, of course," I answered, anxious to bring home a wonderful gift for my son. "I would appreciate your assistance, professore."

With that he led me out of the tiny, crowded room, through the store's snake-like slither, deep into its cave-like chambers, back through a room dedicated to lutes and stringed instruments that hung on the dark walls, back, back, into another recess full of flutes, recorders, oboes, and clarinets. He motioned me to a comfortable, overstuffed chair. I sat down, already somewhat enchanted, while he instructed his young assistant to run next door to the bar and get us each a *caffè*.

In the meantime, he selected seven alto recorders, all made of wood, each a different shade of rich brown. He lined them up on a small, round, mahogany parlor table and described the wood of each instrument, its characteristic sound, and special qualities. As he talked his hands gently caressed the smooth surface of the recorder he held while his twinkling eyes communicated pleasure.

When the young woman arrived with our *caffè*, he thanked her, encouraged her to join us, and proceeded to entertain us with strains of Bach, Vivaldi, and Mozart to demonstrate the particularities of each instrument. Encouraging me to choose the one or two most appropriate for my son's musical style, he exclaimed "Brava, signora," pleased when I tentatively made my selections. "You have a good ear. You have chosen well, and now I will help you make the final selection."

With that, he immediately segued into what seemed Renaissance court music, demonstrating not only the instrument's vibrancy but also his own talent and delight in playing. I felt like a guest in the professor's living room, the private concert a gift from the musician's soul. Thoughts of Orpheus, the magic flautist flitted through my mind as his music filled the resonant space.

I admitted after he had finished that I could not distinguish between the two. I said, "Professore, I cannot decide. The beauty of the music confounds me. They are both eloquent. Please help me?"

"You are correct," he responded with deference, "they are both truly fine instruments. I understand your confusion. But I will play them each again, and explain the sound and help you decide. Relax for a moment more, please, signora."

I listened while he played. In the end logic did not help me decide. I chose one over the other only because its rich tones pulled at me more strongly. Its wood was golden and polished smooth. Fine detailed bands were etched around the ends of each tightly fitting section. Subtle hues of the chestnut grain glowed from deep inside. When I held it, I could feel the warmth of the wood. I imagined Philip with it in his hands he, too, serenading me with delight.

We returned to the front of the store and continued our conversation as I paid for the gift. The professor, animated and content, explained the proper care of the recorder and packaged it for the long trip to California. I assured him as we parted, clasping extended hands warmly, that yes, I would encourage my son to someday make a pilgrimage to Bologna and the music store Orpheus. Then the professor could meet him and perhaps they would share a moment of music. I thanked him for his help and he waved as I closed the door behind me.

I exited onto the narrow sidewalk, the darkness creeping slowly into the medieval streets. I hurried on Via Marsala toward Piazza Rossini and home, the professor's music still echoing inside my head. As I crossed the piazza and reached tiny Via Benedetto XIV, my ears caught strains of music on the air wafting from the inner space of the old city block to my left. The students from the nearby music conservatory were practicing. I changed my focus from the music still resonating in my consciousness to the concert floating around me.

Suddenly the peal of nearby San Giacomo Maggiore's giant bells drowned out the students' practicing. Dong-dong-dong-dong. The powerful sound reverberated in the stone streets and under the portico. As I turned left onto Via San Vitale, the bell towers from Bologna's dozens of churches joined in the chorus. I knew the music of its bells would serenade the city for fifteen minutes. It was an evening ritual I had come to savor.

Their joyful pealing reminded me of the treasures I always found in Bologna: the hidden, seductive charm of her streets and her people. I unlocked the heavy, dark, wooden portone of the palazzo and went in. It slammed shut behind me. The music of the ringing bells accompanied me up the stairs, another gift insinuating itself into my life.

The Gift

Bologna Reflections

Appendices

Bologna Reflections

Useful Information

1. Up-to-date and more detailed information is available on the website for BOLOGNA REFLECTIONS: AN UNCOMMON GUIDE:

www.marytolaronoyes.com/bologna/usefulinformation.html

2. Tourist Offices (I.A.T.) are the best resource to pick up a free city map and to find lodging, tours, internet points, churches, museums, special exhibits and events, public parks, and any other visitor information about Bologna.

- Piazza Maggiore, #6 **Tel. 051/239.660**
- Bologna Centrale Railway Station **Tel. 051/246.541**
- Marconi International Airport (at Borgo Panigale) **Tel. 051/647.203.6**

3. Lodging

- Locating last minute lodging for Sunday through Thursday evenings can be difficult when Bologna hosts its many well-attended business conventions (*fiere*). The number of nights required for booking a room could be prescribed and the price significantly elevated. Planning ahead will allow you to be aware of availablilty and cost implications. Be especially attentive in the early spring for the Childrens Book Fair (*Fiera del Libro per Ragazzi*). Rooms are often reserved a year in advance.

- If you arrive in Bologna without lodging, go to one of the Tourist Information Offices (I.A.T.) listed above, and specifically to the C.S.T. (*Centro Sevizi per Turisti*) desk. Usually an assistant with good English skills will be able to help you find a room in a hotel or bed and breakfast establishment at the price level you prefer. The desks are open seven days a week during posted times. Since a late arrival could make an in-person visit impossible, an earlier in the day phone call or online request would be advisable.

  Telephone Assistance: **051/234.735 or 051/225.218**
  Online Search: www.bolognareservation.com

4. Local Transportation at Arrival

- **Automobile** traffic is restricted in Bologna's city center (Centro Storico). To be allowed access and to avoid a heavy fine it is important to discuss arrangements ahead of time with the hotel when booking the reservation. The other option is to find lodging outside of the city center where fewer restrictions exist.

- **Marconi International Airport** to City Center and/or Bologna Centrale Railway Station

    1. **Aerobus** is a shuttle service dedicated to connecting the airport with the city center, Bologna Centrale Railway Station, and the convention center. Follow the signs inside the Arrivals Terminal to the exit and go to the special bus stop. You can pay as you board the bus. For more information call **051/290.290** or go to the web site www.atc.bo.it.

    2. **Taxi** line forms outside the Arrivals Terminal. Follow the signs inside for directions to the proper exit.

  - **Bologna Centrale Railway Station** to Local Destinations

    1. **City Bus** (AT'C) lines converge at the train station. For detailed information and tickets go to the AT'C office located outside the main door. You should purchase a ticket before you board the bus. Tickets are also available at some newspaper vendors at the station. For schedules and routes check the web site: www.atc.bo.it.

    2. **Taxi** line forms outside and to the right of the main exit.

5. Emergency Assistance

- General Emergency Phone Number **Tel. 113**
- Police **Tel. 113**
- Carabinieri **Tel. 112**
- Fire **Tel. 115**
- Medical **Tel. 118**
- 24-Hour Pharmacy **Farmacia Comunale** in Piazza Maggiore
- Central Garage for Towed Vehicles
    65 Via Gardino **Tel. 051/521.222**

6. Transportation

- Taxi **Tel. 051/372.727** (Radio Taxi CO.TA.BO), **Tel. 051/534.141** (C.A.T.)

- AT'C Bus Information and Ticket Purchase Offices (www.atc.bo.it)

    1. Bologna Centrale Railway Station (AT'C Office)
    2. Marconi International Airport (I.A.T. desk in Arrivals area)
    3. Via Rizzoli, #9
    4. Ticket purchase is possible at many bars, *tabacchi* shops, newspaper stands, etc.

Timeline of Bologna's History

BC

800 Villanovan Civilization exists just to the east of modern Bologna

500 Felsina (Etruscan Bologna) is the capital of the Etruscan Villanovan Civilization

300 The Galli Boli (Celts) occupy the territory of Felsina and call it Bona

189 Rome founds the colony of Bononia

187 Construction of the Via Emilia

88 Bononia becomes a Roman city

AD

BC 27–AD 476 Roman Empire

53 A huge fire destroys Bononia, which is then rebuilt by Nero

313 Edict of Milan: Christianity sanctioned by the Roman Empire

330 Constantine moves the capital of the Roman Empire to Constantinople

330–c.1453 Byzantine Empire

392 St. Ambrose builds the first Christian structure associated with the basilica of Santo Stefano in Bologna

402 Imperial seat of the Roman Empire moved to Ravenna

431–50 San Petronio's episcopate in Bologna

476 Fall of the Western Roman Empire

490–552 Ostrogothic Kingdom of Italy

Bologna Reflections

568–777 Lombard Kingdom of Italy

568 Bologna again part of the Eastern Roman Empire

680 Peace between the Lombards and Byzantium

727 Liutprando (Lombard) conquers Bologna

800 Charlemagne first Holy Roman Emperor

824 Charlemagne takes over Bologna and gives it to Pope Adrian I

898 Bologna and her province are annexed to the Kingdom of Italy and governed by a count

1076–1122 Struggle for Investiture between the Holy Roman Empire and the Papacy

1088 Traditional date given for the origin of the ancient University of Bologna

1100–1250 The Crusades

1116 Henry V pardons Bologna's revolt against imperial power and grants the city various economic and judicial concessions

1154 Emperor Frederick Barbarossa issues the *Autentica Habita* conceding various privileges to the university community in Bologna

1155 Frederick Barbarossa crowned Holy Roman Emperor

1158 Diet of Roncaglia establishes legal position of cities in the empire

1163 Frederick Barbarossa destroys Bologna's city walls

1164 Bologna's first Podestà

1176–92 The city grows, builds new city walls, gates, and canals

1183 The Peace of Constance between the Italian cities and the Empire

1190–1225 Growth of Popular Comuni

1198 Frederick II crowned king of Sicily

1231 Popular Comune established in Bologna

1257 The Council of the People decrees that all inhabitants of Bologna are free citizens

1274 Factional wars in Bologna

1278 Bologna puts herself under the authority of Pope Nicolò III, but continues to be more or less autonomous

1337–44 The Signoria of Taddeo Pepoli, Vicar of the Pope, in Bologna

1347–50 The Black Death (bubonic plague) in Europe

1378–1418 The Great Schism of the West

1390 (June 7) The Bolognese people place the first stone of the basilica of San Petronio, to honor their patron saint and as a symbol of local power

1400–45 Wars between Bolognese factions

1407 Bologna again under jurisdiction of the Papacy

1445–60 The Signoria of Sante Bentivoglio in Bologna

1453 Fall of Byzantium under the Turks

1460–1506 The Signoria of Giovanni II Bentivoglio in Bologna

1506 Pope Julius II retakes control of Bologna, making it a Papal State governed by a papal legate and a local senate

1530 Charles V crowned Holy Roman Emperor by Pope Clement VII in Bologna

1547 Council of Trent temporarily moved to Bologna's Palazzo Bevilacqua in Via D'Azeglio

1555–1619 Ludovico Carracci, Bolognese artist

1560–1609 Annibale Carracci, Bolognese artist

1563 Inauguration of the Palazzo dell'Archiginnasio (Palazzo delle Scuole Nuove)

1572–85 The Papacy of the Bolognese Pope Gregory XIII

1575–1642 Guido Reni, Bolognese artist

1618–48 Thirty-Year's War

1630 Epidemic of the plague in Bologna

1796 Napoleon's first Italian campaign

1797 Bologna participates in the Repubblica Cisalpina

1803 Seat of the University of Bologna moved to Via Zamboni

1805 Napoleon is crowned emperor and king of Italy

1815 Battle of Waterloo, defeat of Napoleon

1814–15 Congress of Vienna restores Bologna to the Papacy

1849–78 Vittorio Emanuele II, king of Italy

1859 Second War of Italian Independence

1861 Proclamation of the Kingdom of Italy

1870 Papal States annexed to the Kingdom of Italy

Bologna Reflections

1878–1900 Umberto I, king of Italy

1900 Umberto I assassinated and Vittorio Emanuele III becomes king of Italy

1914–18 First World War

1922 March on Rome, beginning of the Fascist Regime in Italy

1925–43 Fascist State

1933 Hitler assumes power in Germany

1939-45 Second World War

1946 Proclamation of the Republic of Italy

1980 Fascist bomb explodes at the Bologna Centrale train station

1988 Nine hundredth anniversary of the University of Bologna

1994 Mary's first trip to Bologna

2009 BOLOGNA REFLECTIONS published

Bibliography

Abracadabra: Magia e Malocchio nella Bologna che Fu. Ed. Tiziano Costa. Bologna: Studio Costa.

Bergonzoni, Franco and Giorgio Tambra, *Sulle Tracce di Rolandino* (1215–1300): *Itinerario Medievale nella Bologna d'Oggi.* Bologna: Fondazione Cassa di Risparmio in Bologna, 2000.

Bernabei, Giancarlo and Mauro Marzocchi, *I Portici*, from *Le Meraviglie di Bologna*, Number 5. Bologna: Santarini, 1992.

Bishop, Morris, *The Middle Ages.* Boston: Houghton Mifflin Company, 1987.

Bologna. Trieste: Touring Club Italiano, 1995.

Bonazzi, Gabriele, *Bologna nella Storia.* Bologna: Zanichelli, 1989.

Bulgarelli, Fabrizio, Mauro Baldassarre and Fabrizio Zecchin, *Pianeta Bologna e Dintorni: Guida alle osterie, birrerie, pub, enoteche di Bologna e di una buona fetta della provincia.* Argelato: Editrice Castello del Bentivoglio, 1993.

Costa, Tiziano, Silvia D'Altri, and Marco Poli, *Tutta Bologna: per Conoscere il Meglio della Città.* Bologna: Studio Costa s.a.s., 1997.

Colitta, Carlo, *Il Palazzo dell'Archiginnasio e L'Antico Studio Bolognese*, 3rd ed. Bologna: Ristampa Anastatica, 1987.

De Angelis, Carlo, Renzo Grandi, Paolo Nannelli and Roberto Scannavini, *Introduzione al Museo Civico Medievale Palazzo Ghisilardi-Fava.* Bologna: Comune di Bologna, 1990.

Dondarini, Rolando, *Bologna Medioevale nella Storia delle Città.* Bologna: Pàtron Editore, 2000.

Duby, Georges, and Michelle Perrot, *Storia delle Donne in Occidente: Il Medioevo.* Ed. Christine Klapisch-Zuber. Bari: Laterza e Figli, 1995.

Emilia Romagna Itinerari Ebraici: I Luoghi, La Storia, L'Arte. Ed. Annie Sacerdoti and Annamarcella Tedeschi Falco. Venezia: Marsilio Editori s.p.a., 1992.

Bologna Reflections

Fanti, Mario, *Le Vie di Bologna: Saggio di Toponomastica Storica, - I, II*, 2nd ed. Bologna: Istituto per la Storia di Bologna, 2000.

Farina, Rachele, and Maria Teresa Sillano, "La Pastorella d'Arcadia Contesta . . . il Settecento Femminista in Italia." *Esistere Come Donna*. Milano: Nuove Edizioni Gabriele Mazzotta, 1983.

Ferrari, Paola, "La Peste del 1630" (1997).

———, "San Domenico" (1997).

Greco, Giovanni, "Dai Postriboli alle Case Chiuse." *Bologna: Ieri, Oggi, Domani* (April, 1996): 72–76.

Guidoni, Enrico, and Angelica Zolla, *Progetti per una città: Bologna nei secoli XIII e XIV*. Roma: Bonsignori Editore, 2000.

Il Museo e Lo Studio: sec. XI–XIV. Ed. Direzione del Museo Civico Medievale. Bologna: 1991.

Hazan, Marcella, *Essentials of Classic Italian Cooking*. New York: Alfred A. Knopf, 1993.

Kaspar, Lynne Rossetto, *The Splendid Table: Recipes from Emilia Romagna, the Heartland of Northern Italian Food*. New York: William Morrow and Company, Inc., 1992.

I romani in Sala Borsa: La basilica civile di Bononia. Biblioteca Sala Borsa. Bologna: 2003.

"La Nostra Storia," from the web site of the Biblioteca Sala Borsa: www.bibliotecasalaborsa.it.

Lanzi, Gioia, *La Basilica di San Petronio*. Bologna: Editcom.

Lodi, Enzo, *San Petronio: Patrono della Città e Diocesi di Bologna*. Bologna: Editcom.

L'Università a Bologna: Personaggi, Momenti e Luoghi dalle Origini al XVI Secolo. Ed. Ovidio Capitani. Bologna: Casa di Risparmio in Bologna, 1987.

Moulin, Lèo, *La Vita degli Studenti nel Medioevo*. Milano: Jaca Book, 1992.

Pini, Antonio Ivan, *Città, Chiese, Culti Civici in Bologna Medievale*. Bologna: Cooperativa Libreria Universitaria Editrice Bologna, 1999.

Pradelli, Alessandro Molinari, *Bologna tra storia e osterie: Viaggio nelle tradizioni enogastronomiche petroniane*. Bologna: Pendragon, 2001.

Ricci, Giovanni, *Le città nella storia d'Italia: Bologna*. Roma: Laterza & Figli, 1985.

Riccòmini Eugenio, *Aprilocchio: Un itinerario per scoprire le cinquanta cose più belle della città di Bologna*. Bologna: Nuovo Alfa Editoriale.

Rodriguez, Fernando, "Monumenti della pittura emiliana del '600: Gli affreschi della Madonna dell'Orazione."

Roversi, Giancarlo, *La Magnifica Cucina: Fasti e vicende della tavola in Emilia e Romagna*. Imola: Edizioni L'inchiostroblu, 1995.

San Giacomo Maggiore in Bologna: Guida storico-artista. Religiosi Agostiniani.

Santunione, Giovanni, *Inseguendo un Mito Matilde di Canossa: Storia, Leggende, Scandali, Luoghi, Itinerari per Conoscere la Grande Contessa*. Modena: Edizione Il Fiorino, 1996.

Sartoni, Monica Cesari, and Alessandro Molinari Pradelli, *La Cucina Bolognese: i piatti tipici e le ricette tradizionali di una gastronomia tra le più apprezzate e gustose d'Italia, divenuta nei secoli famosa nel mondo*. Roma: Newton and Compton Editori, 1996.

Stivani, Eros, *L'Oratorio di Santa Cecilia*. Bologna: Studio Costa, 1998.

Una Lontana Città: Bologna 1219–1315. Ed. Direzione del Museo Civico Medievale. Bologna: 1989.

Vianelli, Athos, *Le Strade e i portici di Bologna*. Roma Newton & Compton editori, 2002.

Vianelli, Athos, and Mario Vianelli, *Bologna: Nuova Guida Artistica, Storica e Aneddotica*. Bologna: Libreria Rizzoli, 1994.

Vignali, Luigi, *San Francesco: Guida Architettonica alla Basilica Francescana di Bologna*. Bologna: Grafis Edizioni, 1996.

Zauli, Paolo, *Nel Grande Cuore di Bologna*. Bologna: Industrie Grafiche Labanti & Nanni, 1994.

Bologna Reflections

Index

—B—

—C—

—D—

—E—

—F—

—G—

—Q—

—S—

—T—

Printed in Great Britain
by Amazon

17553422R00160